The playhouse which the Elizabethan entrepreneur James Burbage and his brother-in-law, John Brayne, built in Shoreditch, London, in 1576 and called the Theatre was the first of the twelve that housed a great theatrical age. It was a leading playhouse until 1598 and then, after being dismantled and carried across the Thames to Southwark, became the best-known theatre of the period, the Globe. This collection of essays constitutes the first close look at the Theatre in Shoreditch and its contemporaries since 1923. The contributors discuss the design and use of the Theatre, the extraordinary financial and legal history of the enterprise, and the conditions affecting it and other playhouses of the first generation. Not surprisingly, their findings call in question some of the most conspicuous of received ideas, including the notion that "heavens" were an invariable feature of Elizabethan playhouses. *The First Public Playhouse* prepares the way for a new assessment of theatrical conditions existing in London when Shakespeare became a player and during much of his career as a dramatist.

The contributors are Glynne Wickham, William Ingram, Richard Hosley, Oscar Brownstein, and the volume editor, Herbert Berry, who is a member of the Department of Drama at the University of Saskatchewan.

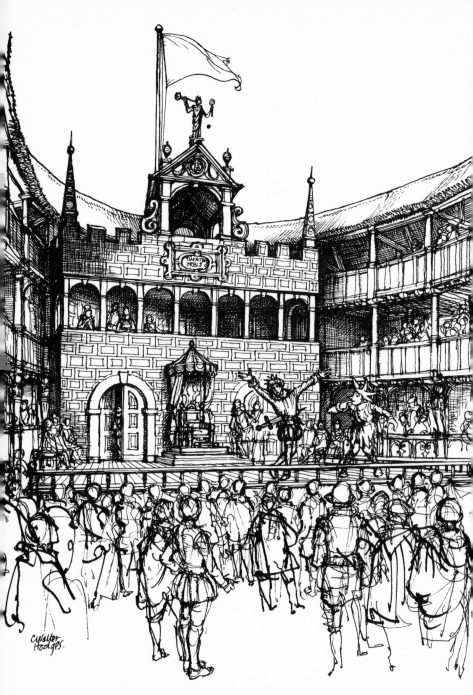

"In King Cambyses' vein"   C. Walter Hodges

The First Public Playhouse

&

The Theatre in Shoreditch
1576-1598

edited by
Herbert Berry

McGill–Queen's University Press
Montreal

© McGill-Queen's University Press 1979
International Standard Book Number 0-7735-0340-4
Legal deposit third quarter 1979
Bibliothèque nationale du Québec

This book has been published with the
help of a grant from the Canadian
Federation for the Humanities using
funds provided by the Social Sciences and
Humanities Research Council of Canada

Design by H. P. Wills
Printed in Canada by Hignell Printing Limited

Contents

PREFACE ix

"Heavens," Machinery, and Pillars in the Theatre and Other
Early Playhouses
Glynne Wickham, University of Bristol 1

Henry Lanman's Curtain Playhouse as an "Easer" to the
Theatre, 1585–1592
William Ingram, University of Michigan 17

Aspects of the Design and Use of the First Public Playhouse
Herbert Berry, University of Saskatchewan 29

The Theatre and the Tradition of Playhouse Design
Richard Hosley, University of Arizona 47

Why Didn't Burbage Lease the Beargarden? A Conjecture in
Comparative Architecture
Oscar Brownstein, University of Iowa 81

A Handlist of Documents about the Theatre in Shoreditch
Herbert Berry, University of Saskatchewan 97

INDEX 135

Illustrations

"In King Cambyses' vein" by C. Walter Hodges
frontispiece

"The Theatre and the Tradition of Playhouse Design"

1. A detail of "The View of the City of London from the North towards the South" (Bibliotheek der Rijksuniversiteit, Utrecht) 51

2. A detail of "The View of the City of London from the North towards the South" (Bibliotheek der Rijksuniversiteit, Utrecht) 54

3. The Calais banqueting house 65

4. A plan of the first gallery of the Calais banqueting house 66

5. A section of the Calais banqueting house 67

6. One of the sixteen bays of the frame of the Calais banqueting house 68

7. A cross-section at ground level of the central column of the Calais banqueting house 71

Figures 3–7 © Richard Hosley 1979

"Why Didn't Burbage Lease the Beargarden?"

1. "The Beare bayting," from Braun and Hogenberg's *Civitates Orbis Terrarum* (1573), 1 86

2. The bear-baiting ring, from William Smith's *A Particular Description of England* (1588) 87

3. A schematic comparison of viewing conditions in a baiting amphitheatre and a playhouse 90

Preface

Because Shakespeare acted in it and wrote plays for it, the first Globe Playhouse (erected in 1599) has attracted universal attention for a very long time. Moreover, it has come to be seen as virtually the sole manifestation of Tudor and Stuart play-houses, and the evidence which survives to describe this or that aspect of the eleven other public playhouses sooner or later has come also to describe the first Globe. What we suppose it looked like, for example, derives mostly from the one public playhouse for which a picture of the interior survives, the Swan (1595), the two for which builders' contracts survive, mainly the Fortune (1600) but also the Hope (1614), and one for which a reliable and extensive picture of the exterior has survived, the second Globe (1614). Indeed, in some of the most obvious writing about the public playhouses, this image of the first Globe has come to be the idea of the public playhouse in general, applying to them all from beginning to end, and inevitably styled Shakespearean.

Yet before the first Globe and its contemporaries were dreamt of, four others existed, and Shakespeare played in and wrote for at least two or three and maybe all. Three were built at the very beginning of the history of the public playhouses and another a decade later: the Theatre in Shoreditch (1576), which was the first of them and the one with which Shakespeare had most surely to do, the Curtain nearby (1577), the playhouse at Newington Butts (1577?), and Philip Henslowe's the Rose (1587). Many of our assumptions about these places have been the result of a wholesale and thoughtless reference to later places. Although a great deal of primary material about the Theatre was printed up to 1913, for example, no significant book or article about the place has appeared since. The time, therefore, would seem to have come round for a close look at the Theatre and at the conditions which affected it and the others of this first generation alike. The essays which follow constitute that close look.

Not surprisingly, these essays may end some of the most conspicuous of the received ideas about the Theatre and the other early playhouses. Unlike the later ones, for example, these early places seem to have had no "heavens," hence no stage pillars and no machinery for flying people and things (like chairs of state) onto and off the stage. Moreover, the design for much of the Theatre and its followers need not have come from the theatrical experiences of James Burbage, its initiator, in innyards and banqueting halls, or from the baiting rings. A strikingly similar scheme, meant for dramatic and other entertainments, was well known in 1576 and was at least fifty-five years old. Eventually, indeed, the builders of baiting rings adopted the public playhouses as their model, rather than the other way round. It seems, too, that James Burbage was an even more ambitious entrepreneur of the theatre than we have supposed, and that most of the documents which record his affairs have been reported in print nearly as accurately as we could wish. These essays should suggest, finally, that however useful the conception of a general, "Shakespearean" public playhouse may be in speculations about later places, it is less so in those about the earlier ones.

These essays began as papers presented to the seminar about the playhouse at the Second World Shakespeare Congress held in Washington, D.C., in April 1976. All have since been revised. One, my "Aspects of the Design and Use of the First Public Playhouse," appeared at the seminar only as a brief oral report of notes which I had made while gathering material for my other essay, the "Handlist." If 1976 was the bicentenary of the American Republic, which the Congress was meant partly to celebrate, the year and, indeed, the month were the quadricentenary of the building of the Theatre in Shoreditch. The seminar gathered on April 21, just 400 years and eight days (or, to reckon New Style and hence more accurately, two days short of 400 years) after James Burbage acquired the lease of the site on which he and his brother-in-law would build the Theatre.

C. Walter Hodges, who has contributed our frontispiece, was originally to have been a member of the seminar, but he had undertaken to assist in the translation of St. George's Church, Tufnell Park, into St. George's Theatre, a work which went on much longer than expected, until, in fact, the week of the Congress. The stage in his drawing is derived from Professor Wickham's essay, and the play in progress is one which could well have passed over the stage of the Theatre, Thomas Preston's *Cambises, King of Percia* (1570?). "Enter the king, without a gown, a sword thrust vp into his side bleeding," as the stage direction reads, Cambises and Ambidexter downstage, Cambises saying, "Who but I in such a wise his deaths wound could haue got?/ As I on horseback vp did leape, my sword from scabbard shot,/ And ran me thus into the side, as you right wel may see." The phrase that provides the title of the frontispiece is Falstaff's (*1H4* II.iv). Other than the writers of the present essays, there were two members of the seminar, Professors D. F. Rowan (who was recorder) and R. C. Kohler.

In all the essays call numbers without further identification refer to documents at the Public Record Office. Dates are modernized. People's names are spelled according to the method of my "Handlist" (see the introductory remarks). Abbreviations in quoted material are spelled out in italics.

We are indebted to the Universities of Arizona and Saskatchewan for grants which made possible the preparation of Professor Hosley's and my essays, also to the Universities of Michigan and Saskatchewan and the Canadian Federation for the Humanities for generous grants toward the publication of the book.

Herbert Berry

"Heavens," Machinery, and Pillars in the Theatre and Other Early Playhouses

Glynne Wickham

Despite all the progress that an international army of research-ers has made during the past hundred years in advancing knowledge of the physical conditions and production tech-niques of Elizabethan and Jacobean playhouses, uncertainty and controversy still surround certain important aspects of both. In some cases, assumptions about physical conditions and production techniques are closely interrelated.

The most notorious of these is the so-called inner stage. For some scholars and critics this physical feature of the stage existed uniformly in all Shakespearean playhouses with all the finite, three-dimensional quality of the Rock of Gibraltar. Others regard its existence as an hallucination as illusory as chimeras, hypogryphs, and unicorns.

Another such area is the innyard as the progenitor of all play-house design of the period, a theory still championed by those who like to view the Shakespearean playhouse as a vigorous folk-phenomenon gradually usurped, emasculated, and finally killed off by an effete court. Yet this notion is no less clamor-ously rejected by those who have come to regard the banquet hall as the *fons et origo* of professional play-acting, and the public playhouses of Elizabethan and Jacobean London as incidental expedients devised by impresarios and speculators to capture the largest possible box-office returns while the chance offered.

There is, however, a third area which has attracted much less controversy, but which is also subject to sweeping assumptions and generalizations that need to be questioned no less rigorously. This is "the heavens" and everything pertaining to them—traps, supporting pillars, machines—and it is this area that I wish to examine here.

It seems to have been taken for granted that heavens existed in all London playhouses throughout the period 1576–1642, including private as well as public or common playhouses, and both the second Globe and second Fortune at the far end of the period, as well as the Theatre, Curtain, and Newington Butts at the start of it. Yet once one ceases taking this for granted and asks the question, "Were heavens an invariable feature of all playhouses?", the awkward suspicion arises that this may not have been the case. Indeed, a surprising amount of evidence immediately comes to mind to suggest that the notion of the invariable presence of this cumbersome commodity in a playhouse conforms better with the dogmatism of twentieth-century historians and critics than it does with the pragmatism of Elizabethan and Jacobean actor-managers.

The sad truth is that, being human, we yearn to be possessed of a single stereotyped ground-plan and elevation which we can describe as THE ELIZABETHAN PLAYHOUSE. The De Witt sketch of the Swan has provided us since 1888 with graphic proof of the existence of heavens in that playhouse. Philip Henslowe similarly provides us with verbal proof in his early account books of the installation of heavens at the Rose and in his contracts with his builder, Peter Street, of heavens both at the first Fortune and at the Hope.[1] It is thus understandable that, given the many references to heavens in the dialogue and stage directions of Elizabethan and Jacobean plays, we should have come to endow this evidence with greater weight than its nature actually warrants. Yet even Henslowe's evidence is ambivalent; for not only did he insist in 1613 that the heavens of the Hope must be cantilevered, thus obviating the need for supporting pillars, but in the years 1591–95 he talks about the heavens at the Rose as though they were a novelty: this information is confirmed by John Norden in his two map drawings of the Rose of 1593 and 1600, the latter depicting hut and flagstaff on the skyline, the former lacking both. And if this was the case, where does that leave the Theatre and the Curtain? With, or without, heavens? If they had existed in 1576 and 1577 complete with traps and thrones, then it stands to reason that Henslowe would have incorporated them into the Rose *ab initio* and not waited some four to eight years before making major structural changes to his playhouse in order to provide them. The costly alterations made by James Burbage over a period of some six weeks at the Theatre in January and February 1592 cannot be ignored. Were these "further building & Rep*a*rac*i*ons . . . to the value of xxx or xl^{li}" just repairs? Or did they include alterations similar to those that Henslowe had just made at the Rose? The coincidence of date is certainly striking.[2]

Still more striking than this is the evidence so sedulously collected in recent years by Professor Berry relating to the playhouse in the Boar's Head. Here is a fully professional London playhouse built without a roof over the stage in 1598, then rebuilt with one in 1599, as though the owners meant to build a cheap and old-fashioned place in 1598 and an expensive and up-to-date one when the first proved financially stable enough to warrant the additional expense.[3]

And what about performances at court or in the provinces? Are we to assume that full-scale heavens with supporting pillars, a trap, a loft, and machinery had to be built in the great hall, the great chamber, or the privy chamber of every royal palace in and around London whenever a play was toward, along with the stage, the scaffolds, and the cloth of estate? If so, then why is there not a single entry to this effect in the account books of the Office of Works?[4]

Nor were heavens a normal part of the fittings of provincial guildhalls or inns.

Finally, there is the evidence of Inigo Jones's refurbishing of the Cockpit-in-Court for Charles I in 1629–30: as with the Hope, no stage pillars, just a trap, or rather sprung blinds, discreetly incorporated into the ceiling, painted blue, and stuck with stars.[5]

Thus the more seriously we study the factual evidence now available, the more apparent does it become that heavens, in the form depicted by De Witt and described in the Henslowe/ Street contracts, were a feature particular to some playhouses and not a *sine qua non* of Elizabethan and Jacobean play-production.

In 1964 I contributed an essay to the Marlowe issue of *The Tulane Drama Review* entitled "Notes on the staging of Marlowe's plays" (since reprinted in *Shakespeare's Dramatic Heritage*) in which I tried to relate the physical requirements of the dialogue and stage directions of all Marlowe's plays to the standard mental image of an Elizabethan playhouse as represented by the De Witt sketch of the Swan. I surprised myself then by finding that far less was demanded by way of stage machinery than I had supposed. First, the fact had to be faced that in none of Marlowe's plays do any stage directions exist authorizing us to assume the existence of a trap at floor-level: the two Quartos of *Faustus* merely conform with the printed texts of all his other plays in this respect. So calculated an avoidance of floor-trap scenes would thus seem to argue a conscious awareness on Marlowe's part that such scenes were to be avoided. We cannot know what occasioned this inhibition in the play-maker; but acknowledging its existence leads us to suspect that the earliest of the public playhouses were equipped with trestle-stages as easily removable as they invariably were at court, and that such stages would of themselves make floor-trap scenes an inconvenient even though desirable element within a play.

Just as striking is the fact that in none of his plays do any stage directions exist authorizing us to assume the existence of stage pillars, or of a "shadow" or heavens resting upon them, or of a trap and machinery for flying actors or scenery.[6]

Marlowe is a singularly helpful figure in the present context because the widest range of dates for the composition of his plays within which we can work is 1586–93. This time-span conveniently divides the three earliest public playhouses, the Theatre, the Curtain, and Newington Butts on the one hand, from the Swan and its successors on the other, leaving only the Rose as a direct contemporary: and it is this playhouse that was twice extensively altered between 1587 and 1595 to make specific provision for the incorporation of a heavens and a throne in those heavens.[7] De Witt, moreover, in his verbal description of London's playhouses of 1596 draws his readers' attention to the inferior quality of the two North Bank playhouses compared to the Rose and the Swan. Speaking of "the four amphitheatres in London" he says: "The two more magnificent of these are situated to the Southward beyond the Thames, and from the signs suspended before them are called the Rose and the Swan."[8] In short, this passage confirms our belief that the playhouse at Newington Butts had by then gone out of business,[9] and establishes as fact that the two relatively new playhouses on the South Bank were visibly better furnished than their prototypes on the North Bank.

Another course of action that is open to us is to examine all surviving documents relating to the Theatre, and all plays which survive written between 1576 and 1591. I have done so, and in one respect, at least, my findings have been very disappointing. First, a careful reading of all the documents relating specifically to the Theatre has failed to supply a single reference to a shadow or heavens or to stage pillars supporting them. Of course this does not amount to proof that they did not exist, only that no one had occasion to mention them. Yet granted that a sufficient number of these documents have survived for C. W. Wallace to have filled 250 pages of print with his transcriptions of them, is this not a singular enough fact to force us to be on our guard against assuming their existence? Professor Berry's essay in this volume substantiates this point.

Turning next to play texts, we again have to accept negative findings. There are only forty-five of them that can possibly be regarded as written for public rather than college or court performance. This total includes *all* Lyly's plays, though it is to be doubted whether some ever reached a public playhouse. These are set out in the handlist appended to this essay. Of the many that must have been written and performed between 1576 and 1591, this is a perilously small residual sample to use for any statistical purpose. Nevertheless, with that warning given, the lack of any direct authority from dialogue or stage directions to countenance the existence of heavens or permanent stage pillars must be viewed as evidence of a kind.

What then do the plays tell us? Above all else they declare unanimously that no posts or pillars and no heavens or machinery for ascents or descents are called for in any stage directions or dialogue before the building of the Rose began in 1587. Thereafter both features begin to make a somewhat tentative appearance, though one cannot be certain from the words actually used to describe the effect desired in some cases whether the feature in question was temporary and particular to that play, or regarded as permanent playhouse equipment. It is evident, however, that Robert Greene's plays are uniformly more "spectacular" than those of any of his predecessors or contemporaries, and it is at least possible that he played some part in persuading Philip Henslowe to spend more money on improving staging facilities at the Rose in 1591.

Pillars and posts

Prior to 1595 only two plays postulate the need for a practicable post or posts, the stage direction in each case being reinforced by the dialogue: *The Spanish Tragedy* and *The Three Lords and Three Ladies of London*, both c. 1587–90.

In Act III, scene 1, of the 1592 edition of *The Spanish Tragedy*, the Viceroy of Portugal, suspecting Alexandro to be an heretic and a traitor, cries:

> No more, I say! to the tortures! when!
> Bind him, and burn his body in those flames,
> That shall prefigure those unquenched fires
> Of Phlegethon preparéd for his soul. (11. 47–50)

This command is accompanied by the stage direction, *They bind him to the stake*. This they are doing when the Ambassador enters and reveals that the real villain is not Alexandro, but his accuser Villuppo—

> Stay, hold a while
> And here, with pardon of his majesty,
> Lay hands upon Villuppo.

—and at line 79 follows the stage direction, *They unbind him* (i.e. Alexandro). Villuppo is not bound to the stake in his stead but is led away to face the terrors of the torture chamber. Thus the dramatist escapes the need to proceed with his *auto da fé* on a wooden stage! [10]

There is nothing here to assure us that this "stake" was a temporary stage property, set and struck for that purpose only at the start and at the end of the scene (it is not needed again); but neither may we assume that it was a permanent pillar supporting the heavens and doing temporary duty as a stake. Theatrical realism suggests the former, since the audience would recognize that no one in his right mind would deliberately set fire to one of the permanent pillars, and thus would be cheated in advance of the surprise element in the scene's dénouement. It is, of course, possible that this stake was not of the vertical kind, but rather a horizontal "spit" of the sort which Foxe, in his *Book of Martyrs*, illustrates as still in use for disposing of heretics. [11]

If the ambiguous nature of the stage directions and the accompanying dialogue in *The Spanish Tragedy* is best resolved in favour of a temporary stage property—stake and faggots—that in *The Three Lords and Three Ladies of London* favours the alternative situation; for here not only is there no fear of a conflagration that could consume the whole playhouse, but there are two posts to be accounted for. In the final scene, Pleasure instructs Simplicity to revenge himself upon Fraud and Dissimulation. The 1590 edition reads:

Pleasure: That his punishment [i.e., Fraud's] may please
            thee the better, thou shalt punish him thy selfe:
            he shall be bound fast to yen post. . . .

Then follows the stage direction,

Bind Fraud, blind Simplicity, turne him thrise about,
set his face towards the contrarie post. . . .

(Sig. 13ᵛ)

This device serves, in effect, to allow Fraud and Dissimulation to escape. The play ends with a prayer for the Queen.

Here then we have a "post," not a "stake"; moreover, we are

assured of the existence of a second or "contrarie post." This argues two pillars supporting heavens as in De Witt's sketch of the Swan more convincingly; but it must still be remembered that this play probably belonged to the Queen's Men, and two posts had to be forthcoming wherever they presented it—at court or on provincial tours as well as in a London playhouse: so the ambiguity cannot be removed entirely.[12]

No other evidence is forthcoming from within the dialogue or stage directions of any surviving play known to have been performed before 1595 that makes the existence of permanent stage-pillars mandatory.

Heavens

Several plays written and performed between 1576 and 1595 present angels on the stage; but in no case are any of them said to do anything other than "enter" and "exit": no machinery for descents or ascents is even vaguely suggested.

Thus, in George Peele's *The Battle of Alcazar*, a stage direction in Act v, scene 1, reads:

> Enter Fame like an Angell and hangs the Crownes upon a tree. (l. 1168)

"Exit" is the only word that attends her departure. Or, again, in *Three Lords and Three Ladies of London* the play opens:

> Enter for the Preface, a Lady very richly attyred,
> representing London, having two Angels before her, and
> two after her with bright Rapiers in their handes.[13]

Even the angel in Thomas Lodge's and Robert Greene's *A Looking Glass for London and England*, a play that does postulate machinery of some sort both below and above the stage, simply "enters" and "exits" on five separate occasions—as do the good and evil angels in Marlowe's *Dr. Faustus*.

Gods and Goddesses, in general, behave no less pedestrianly than do the angels; but there are three notable exceptions. The first can be swiftly disposed of. This is the familiar "Musicke while the Throne descends" from *Dr. Faustus*, which appears

in the 1616 Quarto only; and when it does so, it is surrounded
by some twenty lines of text that are additional to the 1604
Quarto. Both may therefore be safely said to have been inserted
after Henslowe installed the throne in his heavens at the Rose
in 1595.[14] More troublesome are the references to ascents and
descents in Lyly's *The Woman in the Moon* (c. 1590–95) and
Robert Greene's *The Comical History of Alphonsus, King of
Aragon* (c. 1587–88).

In considering these cases we must first clear our minds of
the idea that it was invariable for gods and goddesses to make
spectacular entrances and exits on Elizabethan stages. The
norm is admirably represented by the opening stage direction
of Robert Wilson's *The Cobbler's Prophecy* (c. 1589–93):

> *Enter* Jupiter *and* Juno, Mars *and* Venus, Apollo, *after him*
> Bacchus, Vulcan *limping, and after all* Diana *wringing her
> hands: they passe by, while on the stage* Mercurie *from
> one end*, Ceres *from another meete*.[15]

In short, only their costumes and language distinguished them
from mortal men and women, as was the case some fifty years
earlier when John Heywood first gave them stage life in *The
Play of the Weather*.

Both Lyly and Greene, however, wanted to be different, more
realistic, and strove to attain a more spirited effect. Thus in
The Woman in the Moon stage directions state assertively that
Saturn "ascends," that Mars "descends," "Venus ascendeth,"
"Descend Venus"; but no indication is given how or where
they ascend to or descend from, and at other times they and
other gods, notably Jupiter and Juno, simply "enter." This,
however, is a play written for boys and court performance; no
one has ever argued that it relates at all seriously to conditions
in the public playhouses.[16]

This leaves us with two plays, published respectively in
1594 and 1599, one written by Greene in collaboration with
Lodge and the other wholly by Greene—*A Looking Glass for
London and England* and *The Comical History of Alphonsus,
King of Aragon*.

The latter, like so many other plays of this period, opens
with an Induction. The first stage direction reads:

After you have sounded thrise, let Venus *be let downe
from the top of the Stage, and when she is downe, say.*
> Poets are scarce when Goddesses themselves
> Are forst to leave their high and stately seates
> Placed on the top of high *Olympus* Mount,
> To seeke them out, to pen their Champion's praise.[17]

This prologue is immediately followed by the stage direction,

Enter Melpomine, Clio, Errato, *with their sisters, playing
all upon sundrie Instruments,* Calliope *onely excepted,
who coming last, hangeth downe the head, and plaies not
of her Instrument.*

Thus Greene pictures very clearly in words the visual effect
that he wanted for the opening of his play. That he was less
certain about its technical feasibility is made no less clear by
his closing stage directions.

At line 2086 he specifies, *"Exeunt omnes,"* followed by *"Enter Venus with the Muses, and say,"*

> Now worthy *Muses* with unwilling mind,
> *Venus* is first to trudge to heavens againe.

She concludes:

> Meane time deare *Muses*, wander you not farre
> Foorth of the path of high *Parnassus* hill:
> That when I come to finish up his life,
> You may be readie for to succour me.
> Adieu dear dames, farewell *Calliope*.

Then comes the stage direction,

Exit Venus. *Or if you can conveniently, let a chaire come
downe from the top of the stage, and draw her up.*

Calliope and Melpomene share the last four lines. Then,

Exit omnes, playing on their Instruments.

What is transparently clear here is that Greene has made provision for the separate departure of Venus and the other Muses
in all contingencies. He hopes for a spectacular visual begin-

ning and end to his play, but is quite prepared to accept a strictly pedestrian conclusion if no machinery for an ascent to heaven exists.

The really significant fact is that he does not take it for granted that a sky-car or cloud-machine will be available: indeed, he patently regards it as a possibility rather than a probability.

The play, when printed in 1599, belonged like Greene's other plays to the Henslowe/Alleyn company who, in 1598, listed Mahomet's brazen head (needed in Act IV, scene 1) in their inventory of stage properties at the Rose; and it is at the Rose that we first have factual evidence of the installation of heavens and a throne machine in those heavens.

We have already had occasion to glance at *A Looking Glass for London and England* in the context of angels who "enter" and "exit." It should be observed, however, that on one of these occasions the angel is said to "appear" and to "vanish" (11.972 and 983), and that on the first occasion the stage direction (1.160) is extended in a highly ambiguous manner:

Enters[,] brought in by an Angell[,] *Oseas* the Prophet, and set downe over the Stage in a Throne.[18]

What does this mean? At first glance it seems to indicate that a throne descends from heaven with Hosiah on it and attended by an angel; but that is not really what the words say. Rather, they say that Hosiah is "brought in" by an angel—or, as we might say, "Enters, escorted by an angel"—that the angel leads him across the stage to a throne that is already there and empty, and seats him in it. Whether this interpretation be correct or not, I think the absence of the word "descends" makes it quite clear that no machinery was involved here.

Later in the play, however, we are confronted with the stage-direction,

A hand from out a cloud, threatneth a burning sword.

(1.1636)

As neither the sword nor the hand is active, this effect could easily be achieved by raising into view a wooden cut-out with this device painted on it, or by lowering it on a string. Its appearance is dismissed as a "vain fancy" by the company on stage at the time and may be compared with "the writing on the wall" that disturbs Balshassar's Feast in *The Play of Daniel*.

I do not wish to dismiss or minimize the evidence that the examples I have cited from specific plays written and performed before 1595 provides to substantiate the existence of stage pillars supporting heavens containing practicable machinery; but I do wish to stress,

(1) that all of these examples date from *after* the building of the Rose in 1587;

(2) that *none* exists to make pillars or heavens a mandatory feature of public playhouses built before the Rose;

(3) that when only *one* out of forty-five surviving plays requires two pillars or posts if it is to be adequately realized on the stage, and only *two* suggest the desirability rather than the requirement of some practical mechanism to facilitate ascents and descents, we are on very treacherous ground if we insist on both as indispensable features of early Elizabethan public playhouses.

I am thus forced to ask in the light of this evidence whether any of the builders and financial underwriters of the three earliest public playhouses would have admitted the construction of so costly an item as heavens as an obligatory feature of these structures unless they were convinced that this was so common a requirement among all acting companies of the 1570s and 80s as to justify the expense involved.

My reading of the evidence is that no such justification existed; that no money was in fact expended to this end; and that it is for this reason that no hint of the existence of such a feature figures in any of the surviving documents relating specifically to the Theatre.

By the 1590s the situation had begun to change. Stage plays were becoming more spectacular. Henslowe took note of this and laid out the money to remodel his playhouse to make provision for it. In doing so he set a precedent that others were likely to have to follow. Francis Langley promptly did so in building the Swan. Oliver Woodliffe and Richard Samwell apparently did not when translating the Boar's Head Inn in Whitechapel into a playhouse, but did when they rebuilt the place a year later.

And what of the Burbages at the Theatre and at their "Easer," the Curtain? Confronted with the Rose, expensively remodelled in 1591–92 and equipped with a mechanically operated throne in practicable heavens by 1595, did they make alterations at the Theatre early in 1592, purchase the Blackfriars in 1596 and, finally, move to the South Bank in 1598, in order to keep abreast of the times? Was it worth sinking more capital in extensive structural alterations to the Theatre to bring that old-fashioned building up to the standards newly set by Henslowe and Langley at the Rose and at the Swan at a time when their lease was about to expire and efforts to renew it were proving so acrimonious and the outcome so dubious?

Was it for that reason, among others, that they decided to cut their losses, quit the Theatre, and rebuild with provision made for heavens and other amenities that would make the Rose itself look old-fashioned by comparison? These are questions that I cannot answer myself; but I feel obliged to ask them, and I very much hope that others may be able to supply the answers.

Notes

1. *Henslowe's Diary*, ed. W. W. Greg (London, 1904–8), I, 4, 7–10; II, 46–49, 54; and G. Wickham, *Early English Stages* (London, 1959–72), II, ii, 60–61, 209–11.
2. *Early English Stages*, II, i, 308–9; ii, plate VII, nos. 8, 9; C. W. Wallace, *The First London Theatre* (Lincoln, Nebr., 1913, pp. 69–70, 76.
3. "The Playhouse in the Boar's Head Inn, Whitechapel," *The Elizabethan Theatre* [I], ed. D. Galloway (Toronto, 1969).
4. My word must be taken for this, at least for the moment, since I have checked all entries in these accounts relating to drama; but as the Malone Society is to print a complete transcript of the accounts (edited by R. H. Hill), they will be available to anyone to check for himself.

5. *Early English Stages*, II, ii, 119–20.
6. *Tulane Drama Review*, VIII (1964); *Shakespeare's Dramatic Heritage* (London, 1969), pp. 121–31.
7. See notes 1 and 2 above.
8. J. Q. Adams, *Shakespearean Playhouses* (Boston, 1917), p. 167.
9. W. Ingram, "The Playhouse at Newington Butts: a New Proposal," *Shakespeare Quarterly* XXI (1970), no. 4: 385–98.
10. Quotations are taken from the Malone Society reprint (1592), ed. W. W. Greg and D. Nichol-Smith (London, 1948).
11. See his account of the burning of St. Laurence and Lord Cobham. Of St. Laurence, Foxe (much as Kyd might have done) has the Roman emperor say, "Rost him, broyle him, tosse him, turne him."
12. Quotations are taken from the 1590 edition in the Folger Library.
13. Ibid. The quotation from *The Battle of Alcazar* is similarly taken from the 1594 edition in the Folger Library.
14. Both texts are set out collaterally in the Malone sociey reprint, ed. W. W. Greg (London, 1950).
15. See the Malone Society reprint, ed. H. Hart (London, 1914).
16. One cautionary observation needs to be added here. In the anonymous *Clyomon and Clamydes* two equally abrupt stage directions occur at lines 1549 and 1564, "Descend Providence" and "Ascend." As the earliest printed edition is dated 1599, yet the play is usually assigned to 1570 (i.e., six years before the Theatre was built), it is impossible to determine what precisely is meant or how it was effected, or indeed whether this stage direction was added to the prompt copy after 1595. See the Malone Society reprint, ed. W. W. Greg (London, 1913).
17. This and the following quotations are taken from the 1599 edition in the Folger Library.
18. Ibid.

Handlist of plays possibly presented in public playhouses, 1576–91, of which a text survives:

George Wapull	*The Tide Tameth No Man* (published 1576)
Anon.	*Common Conditions* (Stationers Register, 1576)
Thomas Lupton	*All for Money*
George Whetstone	I and II *Promos and Cassandra*
Francis Merbury	*A Marriage between Wit and Wisdom*
Robert Wilson	*The Three Ladies of London*
John Lyly	*Campaspe*
John Lyly	*Sappho and Phao*

John Lyly	*Galathea*
Anon.	*The Famous Victories of Henry V*
Robert Greene	*Alphonsus, King of Aragon*
Thomas Kyd	*The Spanish Tragedy*
Christopher Marlowe	I *Tamburlaine*
Christopher Marlowe	*Dido, Queen of Carthage*
Christopher Marlowe	II *Tamburlaine*
John Lyly	*Endymion*
Henry Porter	I *The Two Angry Women of Abingdon*
Robert Wilson	*The Three Lords and Three Ladies of London*
John Lyly	*Mother Bombie*
John Lyly	*Midas*
Christopher Marlowe	*The Jew of Malta*
Christopher Marlowe	*The Massacre at Paris*
Anon.	I and II *The Troublesome Reign of King John*
Robert Greene	*Friar Bacon and Friar Bungay*
Anthony Munday	*John a Kent and John a Cumber*
George Peele	*The Battle of Alcazar*
Anon.	*The Taming of a Shrew*
Robert Greene	*The Scottish History of James IV*
Robert Greene	*George a Green, the Pinner of Wakefield*
Robert Greene and Thomas Lodge	*A Looking Glass for London and England*
John Lyly	*Love's Metamorphosis*
George Peele	*The Old Wives Tale*
Robert Wilson	*The Cobbler's Prophecy*
Anon.	*Fair Em, the Miller's Daughter*
Anon.	*Edward III*
Anon.	*King Leir*
Anon.	*Mucedorus*
Robert Greene	*Orlando Furioso*
W.S.	*Locrine*
William Shakespeare	II and III *Henry VI*
Christopher Marlowe	*Edward II*
Anon.	*Arden of Faversham* (published 1592)

Henry Lanman's Curtain Playhouse as an "Easer" To the Theatre, 1585-1592

William Ingram

In this essay I propose to speculate on the profit-sharing arrangement into which James Burbage and Henry Lanman entered in 1585, and to suggest some implications for the management of the Theatre and Curtain. I say "speculate" and "suggest" because our present store of facts is insufficient for certainty in the matter, though too great for neglect. Prominent among my speculations will be the notion that Burbage's arrangement was in reality a means of purchasing the Curtain, and that this purchase in turn facilitated the acquisition of the Blackfriars building. But it will be best to begin at the beginning.

When he signed the twenty-one-year lease for Giles Allen's Holywell property in 1576, Burbage committed himself to spending £200 to improve the existing buildings on the premises within the first ten years. Allen, for his part, agreed to respond to the improvements by renegotiating the lease, again for a twenty-one-year period, at any time within those first ten years. The ten-year period would conclude on April 12, 1586; in the ninth year, in 1585, Burbage came to Giles Allen for his extension.

All had not gone smoothly for Burbage during those nine years. True, he had spent £200 and more, and had erected a playhouse; but he had overextended himself at the start, and then entered into a clumsy business arrangement with his brother-in-law, John Brayne. Their disputes were numerous; argument led to arbitration and then to litigation in their effort to stabilize an ill-starred partnership. The lease itself was repeatedly pawned to raise money, from 1577 onwards. Burbage managed to redeem it initially in 1579, and in that year he and Brayne mortgaged it again for £125 to one John Hyde. Burbage seems to have been in no hurry to redeem it from Hyde; the lease was still in Hyde's possession in 1585, with £30 or more yet owing, when Burbage began to treat with Giles Allen for its redrawing. Allen, for reasons of his own, kept putting Burbage off: 1585 turned into 1586 with no new lease agreed upon, and shortly thereafter the ten years were concluded and the option was void.[1]

Burbage's need for money in 1585 was perhaps no more acute than it had been earlier, but his efforts to improve his position were becoming more imaginative. He seems to have found it easier to be unscrupulous in his dealings, even with his brother-in-law Brayne. Brayne was heard to complain "that his brother Burbage contrarye to his faith and promes [did] purloyne & filche . . . to himself much . . . money by A secret key [to] the Commen box." Brayne also claimed that Burbage "many tymes wold thrust some of the money Devident betwene him & his said ffellowes in his bosome or other where about his bodye," thereby "Disceyving his fellowes" even as he practised to "playe falce" with Brayne. Brayne insisted that his efforts to confront Burbage with evidence of his misconduct were fruitless, for Burbage would merely feign contrition, "saying it was the Devill that led him so to do."[2]

If Burbage was growing more reprehensible in his behaviour, he was also growing more secure about being in debt. By 1585 he had managed to keep their creditor Hyde at bay for six years; if the negotiations with Giles Allen for the new lease had been successful, Burbage might have been tempted to default on the remainder of that debt by arguing that Hyde's lease was now a worthless piece of parchment. Fortunately, Burbage and Brayne were spared the hazards of such a course, for Allen's intransigence supervened; Burbage and Brayne ultimately failed to get their new lease, and were forced to redeem the old one from Hyde and to prepare for its expiration in 1597.

I take it as part of Burbage's growing ambition that he opened negotiations in the summer of 1585 with Henry Lanman, the holder of the nearby Curtain playhouse. The Curtain had been in existence almost as long as the Theatre, and probably with equivalent success. The outward tenor of the proposal made by Burbage and Brayne to Lanman was that they pool their profits for a term of seven years, each party taking half the revenue from each playhouse. We know that Lanman agreed, from which we must conclude that they all saw the arrangement as somehow advantageous; but Lanman was also properly chary of Burbage's good faith, perhaps from first-hand observation, and would not agree to the arrangement without binding Burbage and Brayne more securely for their faithful performance.

Burbage recalled his own side of this agreement in a deposition taken some six years later, in which he spoke of his payments to Lanman as a "grant." He deposed that he and John Brayne did "Joyne in A graunt to one Henry Laynmann gent / of the one Moytie of the said Theater & of the proffittes and comodities growing therby for certain yeres yet enduring / as by the Dede therof maye appere / and bound them self in great bondes for the performance thereof."[3]

Lanman's own deposition, taken in the following year, describes both sides of the agreement and is even more circumstantial: "about vij yeres now shalbe this next Wynter [i.e., Michaelmas] they the said Burbage & Braynes having the profittes of Playes made at the Theater / and this Deponent having the profittes of the playes Done at the housse called the Curten / nere to the same / the said Burbage and Braynes taking the Curten as an Esore to their playe housse / did of ther own mocion move this Deponent that he wold agree that the proffittes of the said ij° Playe howses might for vij yeres space be in Dyvydent betwene them / Wherunto this Deponent vpon reasonable condicions & bondes agreed & consented and so contynueth to this Daie."[4]

Edward Alleyn's older brother John, one of the Admiral's Men, recalled the externals of this agreement. He knew that "one Henrye Laynmann had . . . part of the proffittes of the . . . [Theatre] & so must till Mychaelmes now next coming" [i.e., September 29, 1592]. Alleyn also recalled having seen Burbage make some of the payments to Lanman, "which profittes (as this deponent hath heard the said James Burbage saye) were due vnto the said Lenmann / and that he & the said Brayne were both bounde by wryting to paye the same vnto him / in consideraci on that the said lenmann did graunt vnto them the one half of the proffittes of the other play house there by / called the Curten."[5]

Since 1913, when C. W. Wallace published the documents from which these citations are drawn, historians of the theatre have been in the awkward position of having to note the existence of this arrangement without being able to say much about it. E. K. Chambers conjectured that "the Queen's men proved strong enough to occupy more than one playhouse" in 1584, and that this "may explain an arrangement by which the Curtain was taken for a term of seven years from Michaelmas 1585 as an 'easer' to the Theatre."[6]

This comment, brief though it is, is misleading. The "strength" of the Queen's players in occupying more than one playhouse seems to have been primarily a skill in proliferation, to judge from contemporary comment. The Court of Aldermen observed that in 1584, when the Queen's players had been the only company licensed to play within the City, "all the places of playeing were filled with men calling themselues the Quenes players"; the aldermen felt that the players should be constrained "not to diuide themselues into seueral companies." No doubt the Queen's Men were guilty as charged, but their practice may have been confined to the City innyards, for against the evidence of the aldermen we have William Fleetwood's observation of the same summer that though the Queen's Men were playing in the suburbs at the Theatre, the company in the Curtain was Lord Arundel's.[7]

In any event, the Queen's men presumably managed their own affairs. Had they desired in 1585 to divide themselves and engage a second playhouse, they might have done so on their own initiative, also deciding among themselves how they might share their profits. James Burbage, Lord Hunsdon's man by his own admission, was not serving as their manager, and would not feel called upon to bind himself "in *great* bond*es*" to Lanman on their behalf, or, for that matter, to enter into any arrangement with Lanman at all. The 1585 agreement between Burbage and Lanman must be seen, I suggest, as an arrangement between two playhouse owners, quite unrelated to the possible needs of prospective tenants. Such a position may in fact simplify the problem, for, as Chambers observed, "the relations between companies and playhouses during this period are very obscure."[8]

Somewhat less obscure, but nevertheless puzzling, is Lanman's comment about Burbage and Brayne "taking the Curten as an Esore." We are not certain what an Esore is; "easer" seems to have become the popular interpretation, but the meaning of the statement is only slightly sharpened by this change. The substitution of "easer" invites the inference that Burbage wanted the Curtain to provide relief from some strain or pressure on the Theatre. Lanman may possibly have seen the agreement in that light, but the nature of the pressure is not clear. It cannot have been governmental, for the Curtain was equally subject to such restraints. It cannot have been economic, for while an excess of spectators is proof of success, overflow crowds would seem to require a larger playhouse, not a second one. It cannot have been an excess of actors or of play scripts, for supernumerary players do not need an additional stage unless they intended to perform an additional play, and though an excess of plays might suggest to Burbage a useful possibility for expansion it could hardly have been a pressure on his existing facilities in other than a metaphorical sense. Nor is there help in the standard references. The examples listed in the *O.E.D.* under "easer" are all medicinal or curative in import rather than mercantile. The nearest potential equivalent, "easement," seems more appropriate as a contractual term but is equally perplexing, for it is not clear in what technical sense (e.g., as a right of way) the Curtain might serve as an easement to the Theatre.

Further, the very syntax of Lanman's comment is ambiguous. Burbage and Brayne, "taking the Curten as an Esore to their playe housse" (so run his words), urged Lanman "of ther own mocion . . . that he wold agree" to their proposal to share profits. The construction suggests that the Curtain was already an Esore during their negotiations. From Wallace on, students have taken Lanman's comment to mean "desiring to take [i.e., engage] the Curtain as an Esore," but it may equally be construed "taking [i.e., perceiving] the Curtain to be an Esore," a perhaps undesirable condition to be alleviated by the terms of the agreement. This matter is very slippery, I am aware, but the question must be posed.

It would be useful, also, if we knew more about Lanman. In the sixty-odd years since Wallace's discovery of the documents, no one seems to have pursued him further. At the Public Record Office, however, I was able to gather the following information.

A Henry Lanman appears with some regularity among the various documents in the Public Record Office, where the name is invariably spelled "Lanman," never "Laneman" as one usually finds it in such printed sources as Chambers. "Henrie Lanman" first appears in a lay subsidy roll for 1576 as a yeoman of Her Majesty's chamber in ordinary. He continues to appear among the yeomen of the chamber in subsequent lay subsidy rolls for the royal household through 1602. "Henrie Lanman one of the yeomen of her Maiesties Chamber in Ordinarie" appears also in several certificates of residence issued in connection with the subsidies, from 1590 through 1604. The certificate for 1592 notes that he then lived in the Ward of Farringdon Without; those of 1601 and 1604 note that he then lived at Greenwich.[9]

In 1580 Henry Lanman the yeoman petitioned Sir Robert Cecil for the grant of a lease in reversion; the grant was awarded within the month, to the parsonage of Kynesbury, Warks. In 1593, perhaps in response to another petition, the Queen by a warrant under the privy seal granted to "Henricum Lanman unum valecti Camere nostri" the keepership of the royal park at Greenwich. In 1597 Henry Lanman of Greenwich, yeoman, was one of the defendants in a Chancery suit regarding the non-delivery of certain obligations. In 1605 Henry Lanman the keeper at Greenwich surrendered his grant to the King for confirmation. Lanman's name disappears from the lay subsidy rolls and from the certificates of residence at this point, and early in 1606 "Mr Henrie Lanman" was buried in the chancel of St. Mary Woolchurch Haw, a parish in whose registers other Lanmans, including a Christopher Lanman, may be found during these years. No will for a Henry Lanman has been recorded during this same period in any of the probate courts having jurisdiction in London, but two weeks after the above burial the Prerogative Court of Canterbury issued letters of administration to "xpofero [i.e., christofero] Lanman filio naturali et legitimo Henrici Lanman . . . defuncti." The latter had died intestate.[10]

The bulk of these documents (the lay subsidies, certificates, petition and grant, privy seal warrant, and surrender) clearly refer to one person, and the remainder (the Chancery suit, burial, and administration) quite probably refer to the same person. I would not, like C. W. Wallace, claim to have made an exhaustive search, but I have found no evidence of anyone named Henry Lanman or Laneman in any other context than the one I here adduce. Unfortunately, none of these documents —not even the petition—bears the signature of Lanman the yeoman. The proprietor of the Curtain playhouse, who described himself in 1592 as "Henry Laneman of london gentleman," age 54 or thereabouts, signed his deposition in two places, each time as "henry lanmann." We need the yeoman's signature for comparison with these two, or some other kind of evidence to form an equally conclusive link, before we might venture to claim that Lanman the yeoman and Lanman of the playhouse were one and the same person; the evidence leans pretty surely in that direction, however, and I have no doubt that someone will find the relevant document in due course.

In anticipation of that event, and knowing full well the hazards involved, I want to take the liberty of conjecturing for a moment that we have one and only one Henry Lanman here. Having once made that leap, I shall rashly suggest some reasons for his readiness to enter into the agreement with

Burbage. Let me begin my fanciful exercise by comparing this Henry Lanman to his contemporary and colleague, Richard Hickes.

Chambers, in discussing the history of the Curtain, noted that Henry Lanman, Richard Hickes, and others held tenements in Halliwell Lane in 1581. The name Richard Hickes also appears in the list of yeomen of the chamber in 1576 along with Lanman's. Hickes the yeoman must have been older than Lanman, however, for he is first listed as a yeoman of the chamber in 1559, last in 1579. He died in 1584, leaving no will, and administration was granted to his daughter. We know that "Richard Hick*es* one of the yeomen of her m*aiesties* garde" held the ground lease of the Newington Butts playhouse, and it is tempting to conjecture that the Richard Hickes who held tenements with Henry Lanman in Halliwell Lane in 1581 was the same person.[11]

Hickes's career is perhaps instructive in any event. Having leased his playhouse lot to the player Jerome Savage, he soon turned over to his son-in-law the responsibility for managing the property and collecting Savage's rents. Hickes seems never to have lived at Newington himself; the life of an absentee landlord must have seemed preferable to him. Lanman's own peregrinations from Halliwell Lane to Farringdon Without to Greenwich to St. Mary Woolchurch Haw would seem to argue a similar ordering of priorities. (The Burbages, we may remember, never left Shoreditch.) Lanman may have known by 1585 that his interests lay elsewhere than at the Curtain. He may have been ready, after the example of Hickes, to agree that James Burbage should manage the details of his playhouse for him, only remitting the appropriate revenue from time to time.

The initial agreement was for seven years. If the arrangement was indeed of a managerial nature, and if the relationship was satisfactory—and there is no indication that it was not—it is perhaps odd that it was not continued. The deponents quoted above all speak of a fixed term for the payments, two of them specifying the termination at Michaelmas 1592. No one suggested that the arrangement was to continue. My somewhat more radical suggestion is that in 1585 Lanman, who may have been ready to lease his playhouse, was persuaded instead to sell it, and to sell it for the equivalent of seven years' income—the latter figure to be arrived at by averaging the earnings from both houses. Among Burbage's reasons for wanting the building may have been simple security: the absence of any record of litigation involving the Curtain playhouse suggests that Lanman's landlord, Thomas Harbert, was more tractable than Giles Allen, and this may have appealed to Burbage. In his deposition, Lanman recalled that he was urged by Burbage and Brayne by "ther own mocion" to accept the proposal, and the bonds which he required of them for their good performance further support such a notion. With a comfortable income from this arrangement, Lanman could turn his hand to other matters. The royal grants which we know were made to him suggest that he may have been a regular petitioner for reversions, to the Queen, to Cecil, and others, in hopes of securing a larger livelihood. We know in some detail of the success of his petition in 1590; others may also have been successful and may have confirmed his sense of the rightness of his choice. He no doubt preferred to be known as "Mr Henry Lanman of London, gentleman," like his younger contemporary Francis Langley of the Swan, rather than as the "fellow" who was "the owner of the [playhouse]," as Fleetwood had spoken of Burbage.[12]

One objection to my proposal that Lanman's agreement with Burbage was an agreement to sell might be that seven years' purchase is a low figure, the norm in such matters being fifteen. Evidence for this longer term comes readily to hand. Francis Langley, who held the Manor of Paris Garden, estimated its yearly value in 1594, in rents and revenues payable to him, at £200. Ten years later his widow would complain of its low sale price: "the said manour being better woorth then two hundred poundes by the yere . . . was sould . . . for little more then twelue yeres purchase namely for the somme of five & twentie hundred poundes."[13]

But a playhouse was another matter. Its income was not fixed, and good entrepreneurship might increase it significantly. Henslowe's so-called Diary shows receipts at the Rose of some £450 for the 1594–95 season, and of some £340 in the following season. Fifteen years' purchase at these figures would price the Rose at £6,000, an absurd amount when one recalls that a new playhouse could be built (as the Rose indeed was) for less than £1,000. But Burbage was no doubt aiming at just such profits. It might not be amiss to speculate from Henslowe's figures that the Theatre or the Curtain was capable, in 1585, of £175 to £200 a season for the housekeepers. Seven years' purchase at these latter figures would bring us in the neighborhood of £1,300 or £1,400, a more credible sum, comprising (as it must) the purchase of both the building and the lease.

My proposal, then, leads to the consideration that between 1585 and 1592, while Lanman was receiving an annuity of perhaps £200, Burbage and Brayne—later Burbage alone—were operating two playhouses on the income from one. These must have been years of straitened circumstances. Burbage would have completed his purchase of the Curtain in 1592, and would have had one winter season of full profits from both playhouses before the plague closed him down in the spring of 1593. The plague of 1593–94 was a major watershed in the history of the playing companies, and a near-disaster for playhouse owners, as Philip Henslowe's surviving papers indicate. When playing resumed in 1594–95, however, business was better than ever. The Swan went up in 1595, and James Burbage, with the expiration of Giles Allen's lease drawing ever nearer, purchased in 1596 the building in Blackfriars which he did not live to occupy. It is possible that he raised the capital for this purchase—some £600 for the lease alone—by carefully husbanding the profits of a successful 1595–96 season; I believe, however, that a second source of funds for him came from the sale to his fellows of shares in the Curtain playhouse, for from this point onwards the Curtain is to be found only in the hands of players. Thomas Pope held shares in both the Globe and the Curtain at his death in 1604. In 1611 the Curtain playhouse itself, "now in decay" but "wherein they use to keepe stage playes," was held by Thomas Greene of Queen Anne's Men. John Underwood of the King's Men held shares in the Curtain, the Globe, and Blackfriars at his death in 1624; as he did not join the company until about 1608 he must have acquired his share of the Curtain at that time.[14]

It is difficult, however, to ascertain when the letting-out of shares began. Burbage may have sold shares almost immediately in 1585, as a way of capitalizing the operation of two playhouses. There is no mention of this in the litigation of 1591–92, so it may be unlikely; but there is little mention of the Curtain at all in those voluminous records, so it is not out of the question. Alternatively, and more likely, Burbage may have offered shares to his fellows at some point between 1592 and 1596. If it was in 1595 or 1596, the general theatrical enthusiasm may have spurred their purchase, but by that time such shares may have been of limited value; the building was twenty years old, dilapidated, and of no certain future. A few years later, once the Globe was completed, prudence might well have dictated the selling of such holdings. This may explain why so few players are found on their deathbeds still seized of a piece of the Curtain.

One would wish to know a great deal more about James Burbage's expansion into the Curtain in 1585, and how it affected his operation from that point on. I feel fairly certain that Lanman's action was tantamount to a withdrawal from the Curtain, and that from 1585 until perhaps 1596 Burbage was the owner and manager of both playhouses. This sketch is necessarily tenuous, and filled with conjecture; the present state of our knowledge will allow us no more. But I have no doubt that the materials necessary for a fuller understanding will someday come to light.[15]

Notes

1. E. K. Chambers, *The Elizabethan Stage* (Oxford, 1923), ii, 387; C. W. Wallace, *The First London Theatre* (Lincoln, Nebr., 1913), pp. 151, 167.
2. Wallace, pp. 142–43; C.24/226/11, Brayne v. Burbage. The words are those of Robert Miles, deposing on behalf of Brayne on July 30, 1592.
3. Wallace, p. 62; C.24/221/12, Brayne v. Burbage. Burbage deposed, on behalf of Brayne, on February 16, 1591. Burbage's statement in this deposition complicates an otherwise simple issue. In his answer to this interrogatory (no. 2), he tried to explain why he could not, in 1590, surrender a moiety of the Theatre to the

widow Brayne by her agent, Robert Miles, in accordance with the agreement between Brayne and Burbage made in 1578. Burbage argued that the agreement to share the playhouse was voided by Brayne himself when he joined with Burbage in 1585 in awarding a moiety of the Theatre to Lanman. Burbage deposed that in 1590 Miles came to him demanding "the moytie of the said Theatre and the Rent therof" for widow Brayne, claiming that by the terms of Burbage's agreement with Brayne "the moytie of the Theater & the Rent therof are to be had & Receyved by [the widow Brayne;] So it was indede," replied Burbage; but that was "before Jo. Brayne himself and [Burbage] Did . . . Joyne in A graunt to one Henry Laynmann," etc. This claim by Burbage is the only suggestion on record of Lanman's receiving any interest in the property itself. The other deponents, and the framers of the interrogatories as well, speak of the arrangement with Lanman as an agreement to share profits only. Lanman himself describes the agreement in those terms. I see the weight of the evidence as favouring the latter view, discounting Burbage's perhaps opportunistic claim to have surrendered half the playhouse.

4. Wallace, p. 149; C.24/226/11, Brayne v. Burbage. Lanman deposed, on behalf of Brayne, on July 30, 1592.

5. Wallace, pp. 125–26; C.24/228/10, Brayne v. Burbage. Allein deposed, on behalf of Burbage, on May 6, 1592.

6. *William Shakespeare* (Oxford, 1930), i, 31.

7. *Elizabethan Stage*, iv, 302, 298.

8. *William Shakespeare*, i, 31.

9. The relevant rolls are E.179/69/93, /69/95, /69/100A, /70/107, /70/115, /266/13; the certificates are E.115/242/162 (Farr. Ex.), /243/22 (Grnwch.), /243/31, /243/145, /248/127, /250/36, /251/56 (Grnwch.).

10. The petition is Cecil Petitions 1599, abstracted in HMC, *Salisbury*, iv, 76; the grant is abstracted in *Calendar of State Papers, Domestic, 1581–90*, p. 703; the Privy Seal warrant is C.82/1558/m.4; the Chancery suit is C.2/Eliz./L.11/46; the surrender is C.54/1780; the burial is abstracted in the published register; the letters of administration are PROB.6/7/f.30.

11. For a fuller discussion of the Newington Butts playhouse, see my "The Playhouse at Newington Butts: A New Proposal," *Shakespeare Quarterly* xxi (1970), no. 4: 385–98.

12. *Elizabethan Stage*, iv, 298.

13. C.2/Jas.i/L.13/62, the bill.

14. The descriptions of the Curtain in 1611 are from C.54/2075/no.17.

15. I am indebted to Herbert Berry and Glynne Wickham for suggestions which improved an earlier draft of this paper.

Aspects of the Design and Use of the First Public Playhouse

Herbert Berry

Nearly everything we know about Elizabethan and Jacobean playhouses as buildings comes at random from documents about something else. Seeking information about these buildings is a frustrating business, and never more frustrating than when the building in question is the first public playhouse, the Theatre in Shoreditch, because while many documents have been found about the place, they seem to say particularly little about the building itself, its equipment, and its use. They retail the misunderstandings, miscalculations, probably the chicanery of the Burbages, the Braynes, the Miles, the Allens, the Peckhams, and Thomas Screven with peculiar and depressing persistence. Here and there, however, even these documents allude to the building, and thanks to the sheer quantity of the documents, these allusions are more numerous than one might think. Virtually all these allusions have been known at least since 1913, and most have appeared often enough in histories of the playhouses. Nobody, however, has listed them in one place, and, more important, nobody has pointed out some of the conclusions about the place which such a listing might suggest. If the resulting image of the Theatre is very incomplete indeed, it is also worth considering. Some of it reminds us of what we know of other playhouses, but some does not.

I discuss here various aspects of the building and its use, drawing upon every detail about it which I have found in the documents mentioned below in my "Handlist of Documents about the Theatre in Shoreditch."

First of all, the Theatre was a timber building, as all the litigants and several deponents who mentioned the building said,[1] and it was built among other timber buildings which had existed for a long time and many of which continued to exist. The Theatre depended on these other buildings in many ways. The same phrases were sometimes used to describe physical aspects of them all.[2] At least two workmen worked on them all.[3] At the beginning of the Theatre's history it could incorporate building materials from the other buildings, and at the end of its history building materials from the Theatre could be used in the other buildings.

In addition to timber, the Theatre had in it wainscoting, tile, brick, sand, lime, lead (for gutters?), and at least £40 worth of iron.[4] Possibly 10 per cent of its cost was in iron. It was built mainly by carpenters and plasterers, but also by "wo^{r}kmen of all sort*es* for that purpose."[5] In 1582, a painter, Randolph May, was a regular employee in it, "A servant," as he put it, "in the house Called the Theater."[6] It was eventually taken down by a carpenter and his workmen. Nobody mentioned thatchers or stonemasons in connection with its erection, repairing, or taking down. Hence the tile was presumably for the roof, and it must be a nice question why when they re-erected the place as the Globe in 1599 the Burbages should have used thatch. Hence, too, the brick must have been at least partly for the foundations. A bricklayer who worked for James Burbage said that he built chimneys, but he mentioned only Burbage's other buildings on the property, not the Theatre.[7]

The timber buildings around the Theatre were also part of James Burbage's leasehold. In 1576, when he acquired them, these (according to a carpenter who eventually worked on them and a painter) were "very symple buylding*es* but of twoe storyes hye of the ould fashion and rotten."[8] Burbage had the right to pull these down and use their materials for other buildings. These materials were "timber tile bricke yron lead and all other stuffe whatsoeuer of the said ould howses or buildinges."[9] The nature of their roofs and siding appears in a remark of the Burbages: in 1576 the buildings were open to the weather because they lacked "tyling" and "dawbing."[10] They were, that is, black and white (half-timbered) buildings with tile roofs. At least some of them, as we have seen, had chimneys. James Burbage supplied for the Theatre about £50 worth of "od peces of Tymber waynescott & suche like things," which very likely came from these other buildings.[11] It must be, therefore, a fair guess that the Theatre was also a black and white building with tile roofs.

The Theatre was, as Elizabethan playhouses went, expensive to build. When finished, it was worth, according to the landlord, Giles Allen, £700, and the Burbages more or less agreed with him. According to Henry Lanman, who had built the Curtain nearby, and Allen on another occasion, it was worth a thousand marks (£666.13s.4d.).[12] One might fairly say, therefore, that it was worth £683 plus or minus 2.5 per cent. Like other playhouses of the time, or maybe of any time, the original estimates were much less than the eventual cost. In this case they were about £200 less.[13] Even so, there may be a hint that the finished Theatre was not fully the building originally planned. For a fragment of a lawsuit of 1588 has James Burbage saying that his partner, John Brayne, did not have money enough "to redeeme the said Lease nor had wherw[th] to procied in those manner of buildings wherein he had procured" Burbage "to enter into." Curiously, however, great quantities of timber, lead, brick, tile, lime, and sand were left over, unused, when the place was finished, worth something like a hundred marks (£66.13s.4d.) or £100.[14]

The Theatre was large and solid. After it had been taken down it was called "the late greate howse called the Theatre."[15] One of the old buildings near it was (according to the landlord, Allen) "one great tiled Timber barne . . . verie substantiallye builte." This barn was 80 feet long and 20 feet wide, and it was only a few feet from the Theatre. But though Allen thought the barn impressive, in 1576 it was "Ruynous and decayed," and, as a tenant said, "soe weake as then A great wynd had Come the tenant*es* for feare haue bene fayne to goe out of yte." When the Theatre was up, Burbage shored this barn in two or three places against the Theatre, and these "shores" remained until the taking down of the Theatre in the winter of 1598–99, when, because they were still necessary, they were fixed against the ground.[16] One may speculate about the shape of a building shored in two or three places against a long rectangular one (in 1596, De Witt wrote that the Theatre was one of the four "amphitheatra Londinij"). Whatever its shape, the Theatre was clearly a solid affair. Burbage presently had the barn, as well as shored up, "grouncelled, Crosse beamed, dogged togeather," and cut up into flats.[17] At one point, towards its end, Allen and Cuthbert Burbage spoke about using the Theatre as a playhouse for only five more years and then converting "the same to tenem*tes* or vppon rep*ar*ac*i*ons of the oth*er* houses there."[18] So the Theatre was suitable for cutting up into small holdings—flats, no doubt, like the great tiled barn—and if the houses near it could contribute to the Theatre in 1576, the Theatre could contribute to them at the end of the century.

The Theatre needed repairs fairly often, including extensive repairs and "further building" in January and February 1592, at about the same time Henslowe was extensively refurbishing the Rose. On February 25, 1592, James Burbage had spent from £30 to £40 "w*t*in this vj or vij weekes passed," as a carpenter said who had probably worked on the project.[19]

The Theatre was designed so that it could be taken down and carried away, for in their lease of April 13, 1576, before the first timbers rose, James Burbage and Allen had agreed that if Burbage carried out various aspects of the lease, he could "take downe and Carrie awaie . . . all such buildinges and other thinges as should be builded erected or sett vpp . . . either for a Theatre or playinge place." Burbage included the same clause in a renewal which he had drawn up in 1585 (and which Allen refused to sign).[20] In a sense, Burbage's heirs eventually did take down the Theatre and carry it away to Southwark where they re-erected it as the Globe. Allen said some eight times in three lawsuits that the Burbages pulled the playhouse down and took it away, and two of his witnesses who actually saw the building coming down and being removed said the same thing once each, as did the Burbages once.[21] The matter, however, was not that simple. The building was such that once it was down neither the Burbages nor others would have wanted it all. The Burbages spoke once of having taken away just the "tymber" and once of having exercised their right to take away the "tymber and building*es*." They also spoke once of having taken down and carried away "parte" of the playhouse, and in the same sentence and some four others identified that part as "certayne tymber and other stuffe wch weare ymploied in makinge and errectinge the saide Theator." Their friend who helped in the work, William Smyth, said as much once, and their antagonist, Robert Miles, said once that the place was good for its "tymber and other thinges."[22] Eventually, both the Burbages and Allen became more precise, and then they said the same thing, the Burbages twice and Allen twice. The Burbages spoke of their "pullinge downe, vsinge and Disposinge of the woodde and tymber of the saide Playe house," and Allen said that the Burbages, having pulled the Theatre down, "did then . . . take and carrye awaye from thence all the wood and timber therof vnto the Banckside in the p*a*rishe of St Marye Overyes and there erected a newe playe howse wth the sayd Timber and wood."[23] Evidently the building was valuable for its main members (timbers) and its facings, doors, wainscoting, and the like (wood) and little else. In his original lawsuit, Allen said that in pulling down the building, the Burbages trampled and wore out his grass to the value of 40s.[24] Could he have had in mind great piles of rubble which the Burbages left behind in the open places around the Theatre and which (since Allen did not complain of having to do so himself) they eventually carted away?

Allen said that sixteen people pulled the Theatre down and took away its timber and wood: Cuthbert and Richard Burbage, their builder (Peter Street, "the Cheefe carpenter"), their friend of some fourteen years (William Smyth), and twelve workmen, with the Burbages' mother, Ellen, the ostensible owner, looking on. Nobody challenged Allen here, and Street and Smyth, when given the chance, did not deny their parts in the work.[25] How long these people spent pulling the Theatre down and when they did it have long been moot points. On February 4, 1600, Allen said that they did it "aboute the feast of the Natiuitie of our Lord God" in 1598. On April 26 of the same year, two of his witnesses who saw the work being done said it was done at Christmas, 1598. Another, who did not see the work being done, gave the date as "about A yeare or better as he remembrythe sythence." Then on November 23, 1601, Allen said that the Theatre was pulled down "aboute the eight and twentyth daye of December" in 1598.[26] There would be little problem about the business, except that in the official summary of Allen's first lawsuit about it the people who pulled the Theatre down are said to have entered Allen's premises for the purpose on January 20, 1599. Allen is said to have gone before the court in the Easter Term following, and the lawsuit is said to belong to the Trinity Term following that. In another lawsuit of 1601, however, Allen said that he had filed this first lawsuit in Hilary Term, 1599, and the Burbages agreed with him.[27] Moreover, in 1599, January 20 was the first day of business in Hilary Term—the first day, that is, on which Allen could have filed his lawsuit. It is likely, therefore, that the clerk who drew up the summary used the date of filing for the date of the offence, and that the date of the offence does not appear in the summary.

One of Allen's two witnesses who saw the Theatre coming down put his experience this way: he heard "that the Theatre was in pullinge downe. And having A *lett*re of Attorney from the defendt [Allen] to forbid them: did repayre thyther" where he found the men pulling the place down. Not unlikely, when he heard what was going on at the Theatre, he sent word to Allen "beinge," as Allen said, "then in the Countrie," presumably at his house at Hazeleigh in Essex, and Allen sent a power of attorney back.[28] Presumably there was not time for Allen himself to get to Shoreditch, because he was sixty-five or sixty-six years old and, as he said three years later, "verye aged and vnfitt to travell."[29] Hence the Burbages and their men must have spent at least two days and probably no more than three or four pulling down their playhouse. December 28 was a Saturday. So perhaps they worked over a weekend and into the following week—all, of course, in the midst of the Christmas holiday. We may suppose, then, that during two to four days when the City was relatively deserted, the Theatre trickled in wagons along Shoreditch and Bishopsgate, into Gracious Street, down Fish Hill, across London Bridge, then west along the river, and into Maid Lane.

The main question for us is what sort of building could be designed to be removable, could be pulled down and its valuable parts taken away by some sixteen people in two to four days, and its valuable (and visible) parts identified as timber and wood. The answer must be what the other evidence suggests, a black and white (half-timbered) building, but perhaps one many of whose main members were held together not in the usual way, with neatly fitted joints, mortices, tenons, and dowels, but with ironmongery which could be easily unscrewed or unbolted. Those parts which the Burbages did not immediately take away and did not use in the Globe must have been piles of daubing and plaster, much lath, and perhaps numerous broken tiles and the brick foundation. The Theatre, therefore, would have been a worthy scaffold.

Once he had secured his lease on April 13, 1576, James Burbage and his partner, John Brayne, set about getting the playhouse up and open to the public as soon as possible. They put off doing much about the buildings already there on which Burbage had engaged himself to spend £200 within ten years. They seem to have opened the playhouse to the public within a few months and long before the place was fully finished. Perhaps they opened as soon as they had their main members together, gallery floors in place, and walls up around the tiring house. They then set about less necessary tasks, in the mornings no doubt, and paid for them with the takings of plays performed in the afternoons. By this time Burbage, Brayne, and even Brayne's wife were counted among the labour force. They did not seriously turn to the other buildings until 1582 and after.[30] Obviously they thought that there was more money to be made in plays than in a housing estate.

The Theatre had a "Theater yard," as an actor, John Allein (Edward Alleyn's brother), said, and, as he also said, "the Attyring housse or place where the players make them readye."[31]

It may also have had at least one window, out of which James Burbage called his dead partner's widow a "murdring ho^r," but the window is mentioned only as on the Burbages' "grounde" and could have been in their dwelling near the Theatre rather than in the playhouse.[32] The Theatre also had galleries in which people sat and stood to watch plays, and parts of the galleries were called rooms. It was written into the draft lease of 1585 that the landlord, Giles Allen, his wife, and family had the right to watch plays *gratis* there, or as the lease ran, "vpon lawfull request," they could "enter or come into the pre misses & their in some one of the vpper romes . . . have such convenient place to sett or stande to se such playes as shalbe ther played freely wthout any thinge therefore payeinge soe that the sayde Gyles hys wyfe and familie doe come & take ther places before they shalbe taken vpp by any others." There was a door where a gatherer stood at the bottom of stairs (presumably) going up to the galleries. A witness said that he was "to stand at the do^r that goeth vppe to the gallaries of the said Theater to take . . . money that shuld be gyven to come vppe into the said Gallaries at that do^r." He spoke a few sentences later of "the said do^r going vppe to the said Gallaries."[33] James Burbage should have been alluding to this portal when he mentioned "doares" and "Gates," but he probably meant the main entrance to the playhouse, which, therefore, was sizable.[34] Two of the gatherers at the Theatre are named: during the first ten years of the place a literate man named Henry Johnson, who was or became a silkweaver and was both a tenant and agent of Giles Allen; and after 1586 the widow, Margaret, of Burbage's partner, Brayne, who was also Burbage's wife's sister and therefore aunt to Cuthbert and Richard.[35]

It seems that the scheme for dividing the profits at the Theatre was the same as that at other early playhouses. The players apparently received the money of people who went into the yard and the housekeepers, that is, the owners, Burbage and Brayne, received the money of those that went into the galleries. Burbage and Brayne, and after Brayne his widow, and after her her executor (Robert Miles), argued throughout virtually the whole life of the Theatre about the division of the housekeepers' takings. The notary public whom Burbage and

Brayne hired in 1577 and later as an arbitrator said that the arguments about takings concerned "the yndifferent dealing and collecting of the money for the gallories in the said Theatre for that . . . John Brayne did thinck him self much agreyved by the indyrect dealing of the said James Burbage therein." After Brayne's death in 1586, Burbage allowed the widow for "A certen tyme to take & Receyve the one half of the profittes of the Gallaries of the said Theater." When, finally, the widow Brayne with the help of a court order tried to compel Burbage to share the housekeepers' profits with her, she sent a man to collect "half the money that shuld be gyven to come vppe into the said Gallaries."[36]

If James Burbage shared profits of the galleries with his fellow housekeeper, Brayne, he also shared money with players. The player, John Allein, said that he went to Burbage in November 1590 for "certen money" which Burbage had "deteyned" from Allein "and his fellowes [out] of the Dyvydent money betweene him and them growing also by the vse of the said Theater." Allein identified himself and his fellows as the Lord Admiral's Men. Moreover, Brayne's successor, Robert Miles, said that Burbage gathered money which was "Devident betwene him & his said ffelowes," some of which he would often "thrust . . . in his bosome or other where about his bodye Disceyving his fellowes of ther due Devydent wch was equally to haue bene devyded betwene them." These sums shared with players evidently had nothing to do with Brayne or his successors, who did not claim them. Hence they were drawn from the yard rather than the galleries and belonged to players, and hence Burbage shared them not as housekeeper but as leader of a company of players who used the Theatre. Perhaps the Lord Admiral's Men shared the Theatre with Burbage's company for a time in 1591 as they did the playhouse at Newington Butts for a time in 1594.[37]

Burbage and Brayne put the money from the galleries into "the Commen box," which had either a lock the key to which neither Burbage nor Brayne had, or two different locks, Burbage possessing one key and Brayne the other. When it came time to share profits, the two men would together open the box or have it opened. But as Brayne's successors remembered him saying,

Burbage had "A secret key wch he caused one Braye A Smyth in Shordiche to make for him," with which he "did by the space of about ij° yeres purloyne & filche therof to him self moch of the same money."[38]

Other than the remarks about James Burbage's sharing money with John Allein and other players, there is only one episode mentioned in these documents in which players figured significantly. Two people who worked at the Theatre in 1582, a painter and a yeoman, described the way in which Edmund Peckham had then tried to wrest Giles Allen's property from him (see "Handlist," Category A). Allen's property included that which Burbage had rented and on which he had built the Theatre. Peckham sent people to harass the Theatre, and Burbage had to hire people to protect it. Burbage kept his playhouse, but "the players for sooke the said Theater to his great losse." He seems to have estimated his loss at £30 and to have refused to pay that much rent to Allen.[39]

Because eight people connected with the property in Shoreditch spoke about how much money the Burbages had made or were making with the Theatre, it has been tempting to guess what the place might have been worth annually to its owners. Wallace tried it, for example, and by misquoting or inadequately quoting four of the people he arrived at £80 a year (p. 21). Chambers (II: 391 and note) also tried it, and he arrived at a generous tolerance: £100 to £200 a year. The eight people, however, seem to raise more questions than they answer. Most included properties other than the Theatre in their computations and did not distinguish money gained in the Theatre from that gained in the other properties. Only one made it clear whether he thought of the Burbages as whole owners or half-owners, and only one (another) distinguished the Burbages' role as housekeepers, that is, owners, from their other roles as managers of a company and as players in it.

Four people spoke in 1592 about James Burbage's profits in recent years. Two of these four are the most reliable of all the witnesses. One, the actor John Allein, who belonged to a company at the Theatre, said that Burbage had received for the last five years "of the proffit*tes* of the said Theater & other the premisses to the same belonging an hundreth poundes or CC markes [£133.6s.8d.] by yere for his owne share." The other, Henry Lanman, owner of the Curtain, said that since August 1586, Burbage had received "for his parte of the proffittes" of both the Theatre and Curtain, "one yere w^t another to this daye the some of one hundreth markes [£66.13s.4d.] or fourscore poundes by the yere." Raphe Miles, considerably less reliable than these two, said that Burbage had received for the same period "seaven or eight hundreth poundes of Rentes and proffites growing of the said Theater and the appurtynances longing & adioyning to the same." And his father, Robert Miles, perhaps even less reliable, said that for the "viij or ix yeres past" James and Cuthbert Burbage had received "for the proffittes & Rentes of the Theater & the howses & tenem^{tes} there . . . two thowsand markes [£1,333.6s.8d.] at the least for his owne [presumably James's] parte/ And so moche shuld the said Braynes" and his successors "haue had for ther partes of the said proffittes and Rentes."[40] The two Miles certainly meant to distinguish the Burbages' share from Brayne's, and Allein and Lanman may have so intended. All four probably meant the Burbages' share as housekeepers only. Three of them, however, combined the Theatre with the other properties, and ignored the deal which Burbage and Brayne had made with Lanman in the winter of 1585–86 that the owners of the Theatre and Curtain would share the profits of the two houses for seven years. Lanman, finally, combined the profits of those two houses.

Eight years later, in 1600, Giles Allen and two of his witnesses, the two Miles, spoke of how much the Burbages had made with the Theatre, presumably for all twenty-two years or so of its existence. They gave, however, figures which are grossly low and bear no relation to the figures of 1592, yet all three meant these figures to be impressively high. Had they forgotten how long the Theatre had existed? The two Miles said that "James Burbadge and Cuthberte Burbadge in ther seuerall lyfes tymes haue gayned by the Theater aboue A thousand markes" [£666.13s.4d.]. Allen had "Crediblie hard" that the two Burbages "in their seuerall times haue made" of the Theatre "the somme of twoe thousand powndes at the least."

Another of Allen's witnesses said that the Burbages "haue gayned muche," and yet another, "greate somes of money," from the Theatre. Cuthbert Burbage said that Allen's figure was wrong,[41] and he must have been right to say so, not, as Allen probably thought, because it was too high, but because it was too low. None of these people said how much Brayne had or should have made, nor how much of the money was for housekeeping and how much, if any, was for managing and acting.

When we use these statements, we are comparing not just apples and oranges, but pears, peaches, and pineapples as well, and hence we are unlikely to arrive at really reliable figures. It is possible, however, to blend all these fruits and so to see at least what some of the limits of the figures might be. Let us suppose that all the figures refer to the profits deriving from the playhouse only and owing to the housekeepers only. Let us also suppose that John Allein, Lanman, and the two Miles meant only half the profits of the housekeepers and assumed that Brayne had or should have received a like amount. Let us suppose, finally, that the Curtain yielded exactly what the Theatre did, so that the deal between James Burbage, Brayne, and Lanman made no difference in the profits due each housekeeper. Then, if we take mean figures when people mentioned two, and divide when they mentioned sums for several years, we should arrive at this table of the figures given in 1592:

	Housekeepers' profits	
Source	*per year*	*Half share*
John Allein	£233.6s.8d	£116.13s.4d.
Henry Lanman	£146.13s.4d.	£73.6s.8d.
Raphe Miles	£250.0s.0d.	£125.0s.0d.
Robert Miles	£313.14s.6d.	£156.17s.3d.

The figures given in 1600 produce these results if one divides them by twenty-two: Giles Allen, £90.18s. a year, and the two Miles, £30.6s. Allen's figure could be useful if he was thinking only of the owners' share of the Theatre and only of the Burbages as half-owners. The figures of the two Miles make no sense unless they were thinking as Allen may have been and, as well, meant the profits only for the years from 1592 onward.

Should these guesses be right, one could add the three men to the table above as follows:

	Housekeepers' profits	
Source	per year	Half share
Giles Allen	£181.16s.0d.	£90.18s.0d.
Robert and Raphe Miles (1600)	£190.9s.6d.	£95.4s.9d.

Even so their figures are rather lower than the others.

Because of our first assumption at least, all these figures could be higher than the true figure, but the true figure probably cannot be higher than they are. The average of the two most reliable figures is £189.10s. a year for the housekeepers. The average of all the figures is £219.6s.8d. a year and the average of all but those of 1600 is £235.18s.5d. The range then lies between £190 and £235 profits a year for the housekeepers from about 1584 to 1592, with two conditions: 1) any number is likely to be higher than the true figure and concomitantly 2) the reliability of the figures diminishes as they increase. A reasonable guess, which might be high, would be £190.

If all the figures behind these calculations are imprecise to say the least, one additional figure seems more precise, and it leads to further calculations. In 1578 Burbage and Brayne tried to settle their differences by submitting them to arbitrators. These arbitrators proposed, among other things, that Brayne "shuld haue x^s by the weeke for & towardes his house keeping and the said Burbage to haue viij^s . . . for & towardes his house keping of the profittes of such playes as shuld be playd there vpon sundaies."[42] In other words, in 1578 the galleries of the Theatre were expected to yield profits of at least 18 shillings on Sundays. How often were the players likely to use the place in a year? Between 1594 and 1600, Henslowe's players used the Rose six days a week and, on average, 236 days, or forty weeks, a year.[43] If the players at the Theatre worked similarly, if 18 shillings represents the housekeepers' profits from a relatively full house, and if there were nothing but relatively full houses, the housekeepers' profits would have been £212.13s.5d. a year. At least part of this reckoning is about right, for when in 1582 the mortgageholder, John Hyde, collected the housekeepers' profits towards the money owing him, he received £5 a week.[44] If forty weeks a year is a reasonable figure for the Theatre as well as for the Rose, the Theatre would have been worth £200 a year to the housekeepers. So the reasonable guess above, however awkwardly derived, is obviously worth considering.

One may, then, suggest a few things about the profits of the Theatre with confidence and some others, if not with confidence, with reason. With confidence: during at least the first half of its history, the galleries (the takings of which provided the profits of the housekeepers) yielded about 18 shillings on Sundays and almost as much on other days, so that the weekly amount was about £5. With reason: such sums persisted through the whole history of the place, so that the housekeepers could count on profits of about £190 to £200 a year in the 1590s and also in the 1570s and early 1580s. Such sums, finally, would explain why Burbage and Brayne were willing to let the cost of the Theatre rise to some £683, why Brayne was willing to sell his assets to join in building it, and why moneylenders were willing to lend money on it. It was worth about three and a half years' purchase, or about 29 per cent of capital a year. Yet, attractive as such a venture may seem, it may have been considerably less attractive than Burbage and Brayne at first thought it might be. At one point when Brayne was worried about their rising costs, Burbage is said to have assured him, "it was no matter[,] praying him to be contented[;] it wold shortlie quyte the cost vnto them bothe."[45]

Notes

I give below the place in C. W. Wallace's *The First London Theatre* (Lincoln, Nebr., 1913) where one may find a transcription of a relevant allusion, page first, then a colon, then the lines or item number, then, in brackets, the code number of the document as listed in my "Handlist." The "Handlist" gives information about the document, including the modern citation under which one may find it.

1. The building is described as a timber one some twenty times. See the numerous allusions quoted and cited below.
2. P. 189: 9–14, 29–31 [D-2].
3. Three carpenters (Richard Hudsone, Thomas Osborne, Bryan El-

lam), a bricklayer (Thomas Bromfield), and a labourer (William Furnis) said they had worked on the old buildings, and two of the carpenters (Hudsone and Ellam) said they had also worked on the Theatre: pp. 76, 77 [both C-17], 226–29, 229–31, 231–34, 234–36 [all D-7].

4. Pp. 142: 9–13; 147: 15–18; 137: 19–21 [all C-23].
5. Pp. 141: 6–7; 137: 9 [both C-23]. Three carpenters specifically worked on the place: Richard Hudsone, also called a bricklayer and plasterer; Bryan Ellam, also called a plasterer; and James Burbage. See pp. 71: 14–15; 76, 77 [all C-17]; 141: last line; 142: 13 [both C-23]; 226–29 [D-7].
6. P. 240: 2, 21–22 [D-7]; he made the remark and identified himself as a painter in May 1600, when he was sixty years old.
7. P. 230: 11–25 [D-7].
8. P. 241: 1–6 [D-7].
9. Pp. 188: 29 to 189: 2; 189: 9–14, 29–31 [all D-2].
10. P. 273: 26–34 [D-16].
11. Pp. 142: 10–13 [C-23]; 189: 9–14 [D-2].
12. Pp. 148: #5 [C-23]; 164: 21 [D-1]; 185: 12–13 [D-2]; 277: 19–21 [D-17].
13. P. 140: 1–2 [C-23].
14. Pp. 41: 2–4 [C-3]; 147: 15–18 [C-23].
15. E.134/44–45 Eliz./Interrogatory #9 and the answers to it.
16. Pp. 193: 14–17 [D-2]; 225: #10; 227–28: #10; 231: #10; 233: #10; 236: #10; 241: #10; 243: #10 [all D-7].
17. Pp. 201: 29 to 202: 8 [D-2]; 233: #10 [D-7].
18. Pp. 216: 18–23; 221: 9–13 [both D-7].
19. Pp. 69–70: #5; 70: #6; 76: 20–24 [all C-17]; 104: bottom to 105: 4 [C-21]; 119: 26 [C-22]. See Professor Wickham's article in this volume.
20. Lease of 1576: pp. 191: 1–15 [D-2]; see also pp. 159: 8–15 [C-28]; 167: 29 to 168: 11 [D-1]; 182: 34 to 183: 14; 184: 30–36; 185: 22–24; 197: 17–22 [all D-2]; 277: 11–17 [D-17]. Draft renewal of 1585: pp. 176: 34 to 177: 14 [D-1].
21. Allen: pp. 164: 19–22; 165: 1–2, 6–7, 33–35; 179: 11–14 [all D-1]; 197: 7–11, 22–25 [D-2]; 279: 12–13 [D-17]. Witnesses: pp. 216: 33–34; 222: #10 [both D-7]. Cuthbert Burbage: p. 285: 8–9 [D-17].
22. Pp. 285: 25–27 [D-17]; 185: 22–23; 184: 17–24, 9, 35 [both D-2]; 224: #5; 238: #5 [both D-7]; 160: 33 [C-28].
23. Pp. 284: 6–8, 19–20; 277: 36 to 278: 3; 278: 35 to 279: 8 [all D-17].
24. P. 164: 17–19 [D-1].
25. P. 278: 14–28 [D-17]; see also pp. 217–18: #10; 222: #10 (in both of which Smyth's Christian name is Thomas); 238: #5 [all D-7]; 283–86 [D-17].
26. Pp. 197: 8–10 (where he gave the year as "the fourtith yeare"

of Elizabeth, surely a slip for the one and fortieth year—1598)
[D-2]; 216: 32–34; 221: 20–23; 212: 29–31 [all D-7]; 278:
20–21 [D-17].

27. Pp. 164: 1–17 [D-1]; 279: 8–13; 284: 12–15 [both D-17].
28. Pp. 217–18: #10 [D-7]; 197: 11–12 [D-2].
29. Pp. 74: 15–17 [C-17]; 280: 26–27 [D-17].
30. Pp. 141: 20–27; 135: 4–5 [both C-23]; 233: 28–32; 236: 1–13
    [both D-7]. The Theatre is first mentioned as open for business
    in a Privy Council inhibition of August 1, 1577: E. K. Chambers,
    The Elizabethan Stage (Oxford, 1923), II, 388; IV, 276.
31. Pp. 126: 33; 127: 5–6 [both C-22].
32. After an order of Nov. 13, 1590 (p. 48), Margaret Brayne's people
    appeared several times at Holywell (pp. 95: 19–20; 97: 20–21;
    100: 19–20; 105: 17–18 [all C-21]), two or three of which are
    mentioned particularly, one on Nov. 16, when they went to the
    Burbages' "dwellinge howse" near the Theatre (pp. 57: #2; 62:
    2–3 [both C-12]), and another presumably later, when they tried
    to collect money from people going up to the galleries at the
    Theatre (pp. 97: #13; 100: #13 [both C-21]; 114: #2; 125: #2
    [both C-22]). Raphe Miles made the remark about the window
    as an eye witness (p. 121: 13–17 [C-22]), but he added that he
    was not present when they tried to collect money for the gal-
    leries (pp. 119: #9; 122: #9 [both C-22]).
33. Pp. 177: 34 to 178: 5 [D-1]; 97–98: #13 [C-21]; 114: 16–20, 31–32
    [C-22]. Referring to a remark by Samuel Kiechel (a visitor to
    London in 1585), Chambers added that the Theatre had three
    galleries, and he may well have been right. Kiechel, however,
    did not specifically mention the Theatre. He wrote, "There are
    some peculiar houses, which are so made as to have about three
    galleries over one another." See Chambers, II, 393, 358.
34. Pp. 112: 19–21; 117: 28–29; 119: 3–4; 123: 11–12; 124: 26
    [all C-22].
35. Pp. 105: 6–8 [C-21]; 222: 3–4 [D-7].
36. Pp. 152: 1–6 [C-23]; 105: 1–2 [C-21]; 114: 15–20 [C-22]. More-
    over, in "The Sharers Papers" of 1635, Cuthbert and Richard
    Burbage said as much: Chambers, II, 384, 393.
37. Pp. 101: 14–17, 21 [C-21]; 129: #7; 142: 28–34 [both C-23];
    Chambers, II, 140–41.
38. In a question, Margaret Brayne implied that the money in the
    box was to be shared with both the players and her husband.
    In his answer to it, however, Robert Miles seems to distinguish
    between money in the box, which belonged to Burbage and
    Brayne, and other money not in the box, which belonged to Bur-
    bage and the players: pp. 129: #7; 142–43: #7 [both C-23].
39. Pp. 201: 5–18 [D-2]; 224–25: #6; 240: #6; 242: #6 [all D-7]. Cuth-
    bert Burbage's and his witnesses' remarks about the Peckham
    episode seem to be a response to Allen's charge that the Bur-

bages still owed him £30 in rent (pp. 193: 3–5 [D-2]; 207: #3 [D-7]).
40. Pp. 102: #14 [C-21]; 150: #19 [C-23]; 106: 1–6 [C-21]; 146: 32 to 147: 6 [C-23].
41. Pp. 263: #6; 266: #6 [both D-7]; 198: 18–19 [D-2]; 217: #9; 222: #9 [both D-7]; 205: 3–5 [D-2].
42. Pp. 116: #2; 119: 29 to 120: 3 [both C-22].
43. So Chambers worked out the figures in Henslowe's Diary, except that he divided the six years into two periods of three years each, 1594–97 (126 weeks, 728 performances), 1597–1600 (115 weeks, fewer than 690 days): II, 141–42, 159–60.
44. Pp. 52: #7; 55: #7 [both C-10].
45. P. 140: 1–12 [C-23].

The Theatre and the Tradition of Playhouse Design

Richard Hosley

The Theatre, first of the London "public" playhouses, was situated in Shoreditch about half a mile to the north of Bishopsgate and just east of Finsbury Fields; the exact site has been established as lying in the angle formed by the meeting of modern Curtain Road and New Inn Yard.[1] Unfortunately we do not, as we do in the cases of the Swan, the first Fortune, the second Globe, and the Hope, have detailed and reliable information about the design of the Theatre. What evidence we have may be arranged in three classes: contemporary allusions, records of litigation, and a pictorial representation of the playhouse in a panoramic view of London. After discussing this evidence I shall relate the known general characteristics of the Theatre to the tradition of later Elizabethan and Jacobean public playhouses; and I shall direct attention to an earlier tradition, represented by the temporary banqueting house built by Henry VIII in Calais in 1520, which may have influenced the design of the Theatre in 1576.

The Theatre was not a square or rectangular playhouse like the Fortune or the Boar's Head but a round playhouse like the

Swan or the second Globe—by "round" being meant, as usually in the case of a timber-framed building 65 or more feet in diameter, "built to a ground plan in the shape of a polygon having a large number of sides, such as sixteen, eighteen, twenty, or twenty-four." The round form is indicated by the fact that the Dutch observer Johannes de Witt, in notes made during a visit to London about 1596, uses the word *amphitheatra* for the four London playhouses of the time: the Rose and the Swan to the south of the Thames, the Theatre and the Curtain outside the walls of the city to the north. The Theatre may have had three galleries, for the German traveller Samuel Kiechel tells us in 1585 that the London playhouses (including, apparently, not only the Theatre and the Curtain but also innyard playhouses such as the Bel Savage and the Cross Keys) have "ettwann drey genng ob ein ander" ("in some instances three galleries one over another"). In addition, we know that the Theatre was richly decorated. In 1578 John Stockwood, in a sermon delivered at Paul's Cross, knows not how he "might with the godly learned especially more discommend the gorgeous playing place erected in the fields, than to term it, as they please to have it called, a 'theatre'." In 1579 Gabriel Harvey intimates that he may be asked by the players to write an interlude or comedy "fit for the Theatre or some other painted stage." In 1577 the preacher Thomas White, again at Paul's Cross, calls the Theatre and the Curtain "sumptuous theatre houses." And in 1583 the Puritan pamphleteer Philip Stubbs characterizes the same two playhouses as "Venus' palaces."[2]

Information about several physical features of the Theatre is provided by surviving records of litigation involving persons connected in one way or another with the playhouse or its affairs. Since these records are discussed in detail by Professor Berry elsewhere in this volume, I here treat only their implications for playhouse design.

1. The Theatre had "galleries," the number of which may have been three as we gather from Kiechel's statement quoted above.[3]

2. The Theatre also had "upper rooms," presumably the sec-

tions (corresponding to the bays of the playhouse frame) into which the galleries were divided by low partitions, like the "rooms" called for in the Hope contract of 1613: "the partitions between the rooms as they are at the said playhouse called the Swan"; or like the "twopenny rooms" called for in the Fortune contract of 1600.[4]

3. Access to the galleries of the Theatre was, according to one deponent, by way of a "door" that went "up to" or "up into" the galleries. The phrasing implies stairs, and the fact of a door indicates that the stairs in question were enclosed—as indeed stairs must be if access to the galleries they serve is to be controlled by gatherers for the sake of efficient collection of admission fees. The question to which the deponent was responding mentions placing "collectors *at the doors* of the said Theatre." Though Professor Berry has a somewhat different explanation of the phrase, I conclude it means that the Theatre had at least two sets of enclosed stairs leading up to the galleries. Presumably the sets of stairs were enclosed in external staircases like those called for in the Hope contract: "two staircases without and adjoining to the said playhouse in such convenient places as shall be most fit and convenient for the same to stand upon, and of such largeness and height as the said staircases of the said playhouse called the Swan now are or be"; or like those depicted by Wenzel Hollar in his representation of the second Globe and the Hope in the Long Bird's-Eye View of London (1647).[5]

4. The Theatre had a "yard" or "theatre yard." Here the word "theatre" may designate the playhouse of that name, may mean (as frequently) "playhouse," or may mean (as occasionally) "stage." I assume it is the name of the playhouse that is in question, the deponent wishing to make clear that he meant the yard of the Theatre as opposed to that of the Curtain, the last playhouse mentioned (in the preceding sentence). Presumably the yard of the Theatre was more or less comparable (depending on the ground plan of the containing playhouse frame) to the yard of the Swan as depicted in the De Witt drawing of the interior of that playhouse (c. 1596).[6]

5. The Theatre had an "attiring-house or place where the players make them ready."[7] Presumably the attiring-house of

the Theatre was comparable to the *mimorum aedes* shown in the De Witt drawing of the Swan Playhouse. Thus it would have had two large doors giving upon the stage and, in the second story, a range of spectators' rooms or boxes (the "boxes" of "the Lord's room," as Dekker refers to them in *The Gull's Hornbook*, 1609).[8] Alternatively, the Theatre tiring-house may have had three stage doors; if so, the arrangement would be generally comparable to that of the tiring-house depicted by Inigo Jones in his drawings (preserved at Worcester College, Oxford) of an unnamed Jacobean "private" playhouse.[9]

It is notable that the documents of litigation contain no reference to the stage of the Theatre. Presumably the Theatre stage was rectangular, like that of the booth stage which most investigators postulate as the immediate ancestor of the Elizabethan playhouse stage; and presumably also its size was more or less comparable (depending on the size of the containing playhouse frame) to that called for in the Fortune contract: 43 feet wide by 27 feet 6 inches deep, the first of these dimensions being explicitly stated, the second being an inference from the requirement that the Fortune stage extend to "the middle" of a playhouse yard specified as 55 feet square. In addition, we may suppose that, as Joseph Quincy Adams suggested, the stage of the Theatre, unlike that of the Hope, was a permanent one (that is, not a removable one), for, although the Theatre was occasionally used for nontheatrical entertainment such as fencing, there is no evidence that it was ever used for animal-baiting.[10]

Additional information about the Theatre is afforded by its representation in an undated and anonymous panoramic view of London entitled "The View of the City of London from the North towards the South," an engraving preserved in the library of the Rijksuniversiteit of Utrecht. In 1954 Leslie Hotson identified the depicted playhouse building as the Curtain, on the assumption that the Utrecht view is to be dated after the building of the Fortune in 1600.[11] In 1964, however, Sidney Fisher identified it as the Theatre, on the assumption that the view is to be dated before the removal of the Theatre at the

1. A detail of "The View of the City of London from the
North towards the South" showing the Theatre on the
left and the supposed flag of the Curtain Playhouse on
the right (*Bibliotheek der Rijksuniversiteit, Utrecht*).

end of 1598 (Fig. 1). More specifically, Fisher points out that
about 4 degrees to the right of the fully depicted playhouse
there is shown a flag which may be identified as that of the
Curtain Playhouse if the fully depicted playhouse building on
the left is identified as the Theatre—4 degrees being the angle
subtended by the 200 yards separating the two playhouses
when plotted from an artist's point of view established by
Fisher as about one and a half miles west-northwest of the
two playhouses.[12] And he shows, further, that the deduced
point of view produces more accurate (and for that matter very
accurate) bearings of depicted buildings with known sites such

as the Tower of London, St. Paul's Cathedral, and Westminster Abbey if the fully depicted playhouse building is identified as the Theatre than it does if that building is identified as the Curtain. In my judgment Fisher has proposed an essentially sound theory.

The theory is not, however, without attendant difficulties. The Utrecht view appears to show only the roof of the Curtain hut together with a flagstaff stepped from midpoint of the ridge. Presumably the playhouse frame was masked by houses intervening between the site of the playhouse and the artist's point of view. But the depicted placement of the flagstaff is not practicable since it fails to allow for a station at the foot of the staff from which to raise and lower the flag. (At the Theatre a cupola appears to have been provided to accommodate this need.) In addition, the roof in question seems too large for that of a playhouse hut, for it is drawn twice as large as the hut of the nearby Theatre. Is it possible that this roof may have been intended to represent not that of the Curtain hut but that of an intervening building? If so, the roof of the Curtain hut may not be depicted at all, the hut as well as the playhouse frame having been masked by intervening three- or four-story houses possibly sited at slightly higher elevations than that of the playhouse; or the roof depicted immediately behind the flagstaff may be intended for that of the Curtain hut, the staff being stepped from the base of the hut and rising along the face of the gable-end so as to make allowance, at the elevation of the hut floor, for a station outside the hut from which to fly the flag. (Such a station, according to the De Witt drawing, was apparently provided at the Swan.) In either case, as also in the case of Fisher's interpretation, we must assume masking by intervening buildings; and in all three cases, in view of the artist's integrity in refusing to exaggerate his vertical field of vision,[13] we may suppose that the artist remained faithful to his adopted point of view despite the fact that it forced him to show only the flagstaff of the playhouse or only the playhouse hut and flagstaff. The difficulty is further compounded, in all three cases, by the possibility that the artist's intentions were not fully understood by the engraver—

assuming, as we may, that artist and engraver were two different persons.

In any case, I accept Fisher's identification of the fully depicted playhouse building of the Utrecht view as the Theatre.
Fisher's argument from the evidence of bearings is strong; and,
in light of his well-supported point that flags are extremely
rare in panoramic views of the period (including this one),[14]
it would seem to be a coincidence too great to swallow that a
flag practically as large as that of a nearby playhouse should
have been flown from an ordinary domestic building at precisely the point where, in the alternative interpretation, a bearing from the artist's deduced point of view to the known site
of the Curtain indicates that a second playhouse was located.

The representation of the Theatre in the Utrecht view of
London affords the following information about that playhouse
(see Fig. 2).

1. The playhouse frame of the Theatre was built to a ground
plan in the shape of a polygon. This is what we should expect
in a "round" building constructed of timber, for, although bres-
sumers (horizontal beams in the outer wall of a building) could
have been shaped so as to produce a fully round building, no
one working under pressure of a normal concern for costs
would have taken the very considerable trouble so to shape
them.

2. There is no reliable evidence indicating the exact number
of sides or faces of the Theatre frame. (Presumably it was a
large number, such as sixteen, eighteen, twenty, or twenty-
four.) The number of sides depicted in the Utrecht view appears to be eight. However, I take this number to be not a
literally true statement but rather as resulting from a convention frequently used in the representation of large polygonal
buildings at a small size: the artist depicts a small, hence conveniently representable, number of sides (usually eight) so as to
convey the information that the building is polygonal while
unavoidably misrepresenting the precise number of sides in
question and obscuring the fact that the building gives the impression of being "round." An alternative convention, also fre-

2. A detail of "The View of the City of London from the North towards the South" showing the Theatre (*Bibliotheek der Rijksuniversiteit, Utrecht*).

quently used, is to draw the polygonal building fully round so as to indicate that it gives the impression of being "round" while unavoidably suppressing the information that it is actually polygonal.[15] The first convention is nicely illustrated in various representations of the Swan which depict the frame of that playhouse as having, respectively, six, eight, and twelve sides, for the De Witt drawing suggests that twenty-four sides are actually in question.[16]

3. The Theatre had two external staircases, here depicted as standing one on either side of the playhouse frame. Thus the pictorial evidence correlates with the verbal evidence cited above suggesting that the Theatre had at least two sets of enclosed stairs leading up to the galleries. The Theatre staircases

evidently correspond to the "two staircases without and adjoining to the said playhouse" called for in the Hope contract;
and were presumably similar to the external staircases depicted by Hollar in his representation of the second Globe and
the Hope in the Long Bird's-Eye View of London.

4. The line defining the top of the Theatre frame and its
attached staircases in the Utrecht view is, in my opinion, un-
intelligible except on the assumption that the engraver inad-
vertently omitted the peaked roof which presumably, as at the
second Globe and the Hope, covered all three structures.[17]

5. The Utrecht view shows windows in each of the three
visible faces of the Theatre frame and in the visible face of
each staircase.

6. The windows shown in the Utrecht view indicate that
the Theatre was a three-story building. The pictorial evidence
thus confirms what Samuel Kiechel's statement (quoted above)
only suggests, namely that the Theatre had three galleries
superimposed one above another.

7. A door is depicted in the frame at ground level. In respect
of the door's location the artist seems to have combined two
different points of view. Viewed in relation to the staircases,
the door appears to be located in a bay of the frame lying in
front of the stage on an axis of the frame running at right
angles to the front of the stage; thus the door may be interpreted as a single main entrance to the yard located directly
in front of the stage.[18] On the other hand, viewed in relation
to the superstructure hut, the door appears to be located in a
bay of the frame lying in front of and to the side of the stage
on an axis of the frame running at an angle of about 45 degrees
to the front of the stage; thus the door may be interpreted
as one of two main entrances to the yard located in front of
and on either side of the stage.

8. The frame of the Theatre was surmounted by a hut with a
gabled roof.[19] Presumably the hut lay in part over the stage,
one of its functions being to house suspension-gear for flying
effects.

9. The Theatre hut was in turn surmounted by a cupola or
tower of some sort from which rose a flagstaff. Presumably a
major function of the cupola was to provide a station at the

foot of the flagstaff from which a playhouse functionary might conveniently raise and lower the flag indicating a "play day."

Our evidence permits us to observe several significant similarities between the Theatre (1576) and later public playhouses about which we have information on the points in question. (1) The Theatre, like the Rose (c. 1587), the Swan (1595), the first Globe (1599), the second Globe (1614), and the Hope (1614), was a "round" building constructed to a ground plan in the shape of a polygon having, presumably, a large number of sides such as sixteen, eighteen, twenty, or twenty-four. (2) The Theatre, like the Swan, the first Globe, the first Fortune (1600), the second Globe, and the Hope, was a three-story building, hence presumably had three galleries superimposed one above another. (3) The Theatre, like the first Globe, the first Fortune, the second Globe, and the Hope, had two external staircases attached to the playhouse frame and providing access to the galleries. And (4), the Theatre, like the Rose, the Swan, the first Globe, and the second Globe, had (at least by the 1590s) a superstructure hut that presumably lay in part over the stage and served in part to house suspension-gear for flying effects. It seems clear that, in respect of each of these four architectural characteristics, the later public playhouses must have been either directly influenced by the Theatre, or built in a tradition originating with the Theatre, or built in a tradition which also influenced the Theatre.

In respect of one particular architectural characteristic the Theatre may have had a special influence. Both the first and second Globe were like the Theatre in having a cupola above the superstructure hut,[20] whereas it is clear from pictorial evidence that neither the Rose nor the Swan had such a cupola. (The Hope did not have a hut, and evidence on the question is lacking for other playhouses.) Accordingly, we may suppose that the cupola of the Theatre was a convenience and an ornament which the Lord Chamberlain's Men, in playing at the Theatre from 1594 to 1597, found especially attractive and therefore perpetuated in constructing the first Globe in 1599 and (as the King's Men) the second Globe in 1614.

In December of 1598 the Theatre was dismantled by the carpenter Peter Street and, its "timber and wood" having been transported across London to Bankside, rebuilt as the first Globe by the Lord Chamberlain's Men in the spring of 1599.[21] The work of construction, directed presumably by Street, appears to have proceeded with dispatch, for the new playhouse is referred to as "de novo edificata" in a document of May 16, 1599.[22]

How would Peter Street have used the dismantled timbers of the Theatre in constructing the first Globe? This question has been carefully studied by Irwin Smith, to whose discussion I am indebted in what follows.[23]

The first consideration in using the timbers of an old building in the construction of a new one was that the dismantled timbers almost inevitably had to be reassembled in their original relationships one to another. The reason for this was that the timbers, not being held together by steel bolts as they would be in modern heavy-timber construction, were held together by joints cut by a joiner in the ends of the timbers. Each mortise and tenon, since cut by hand with chisel and saw, was unique; and as a result the joint of a given timber would fit no corresponding joint other than that of the timber for which it had been intended as a mate. Elizabethan builders were fully cognizant of this problem, since it obtained also in new construction. The joiner, on the ground, laid out a given pair of timbers that were to be joined together and cut the required mortise and tenon to fit; and the carpenter, when the timbers had been carried to the job and raised into position, would bring each pair of timbers together in the same relationship as the joiner had used when cutting the joints. In order that the carpenter might associate matched joints easily and without time-wasting error, the joiner incised, with a sort of chisel, the same "carpenter's mark" (a Roman numeral or some similar code) on the side of each of the two timbers to be joined, each identical mark being made, of course, at a point near where mortise and tenon came together. Since the carpenter's marks remained incised in the timbers, they were sometimes put to a second use, years later, in making possible the correct reassembly of dismantled timbers that were being re-used in the construction of a new building.

Could the timbers of an old building have been used in the construction of a new one without being reassembled in their original relationships? Smith discusses the possibility:

> Peter Street . . . must either have re-used the Theatre's timbers in their original relationships, or he must have cut off their jointed ends and started afresh with new joinery. But this would have involved not merely the expenditure of time and labour, but also the shortening of every timber in the frame by, let us say, 8 inches at either end. And 8 inches must be regarded as a minimum allowance. We are not here concerned with an average, for the longest distance by which any timber in a given sequence would have to be shortened is the amount by which every other parallel timber in the sequence would have to be cut down. If we accept 8 inches for purposes of discussion (and I think it would more probably have had to be 12 or 15), then every vertical support would have had to be shortened by 16 inches, every gallery lowered by that distance, and the height of the playhouse from first-gallery floor to eaves-line would have been reduced by 4 feet, with, of course, a comparable scaling down of all the lateral dimensions of the frame. It is inconceivable that Street should have resorted to this time-consuming, labour-consuming, space-consuming expedient, if an alternative course were open to him. (pp. 115–16)

Smith's conclusion seems inescapable: "the basic frame of the Globe must have been, piece-for-piece and timber-for-timber, the same as the basic frame of the Theatre." But we can go further. Smith's argument indicates the great unlikelihood that the Theatre would have been rebuilt smaller. Could it have been rebuilt larger? If a rectangular ground plan were in question, new bays could have been inserted in the "received" frame at almost any point, the whole structure thus being readily enlarged without alteration of the four-sided character of its original ground plan. But since the ground plan of the Theatre was polygonal, rebuilding at a larger size could not well have been undertaken, for the insertion of additional bays in the received frame would have enlarged the number of sides of the polygon and thus diminished the angles at which horizontal timbers of the frame met one another; with the result of course that the joints of the received timbers would have failed to fit. If the diminution of angle were small—say 4½ degrees as in the case of enlargement from a sixteen-sided ground plan (in which the "angle of return" at each corner of the building is 22½ degrees) to a twenty-sided one (angle of return 18 degrees)—the joints could have been forced to fit, after a fashion, by slightly reducing the size of each tenon in its vertical planes or similarly enlarging that of each mortise; but the fit of each joint would thus have been loosened in a way that (presumably) no reliable builder would have permitted. On balance it seems to me most unlikely that the Theatre would have been rebuilt larger.

Smith's argument and that which I have added to it suggest that the frame of the first Globe was of the same height, diameter, and shape of ground plan as that of the Theatre. This conclusion does not, admittedly, contribute very much to our knowledge of the Theatre since we know so little about the first Globe. But it leads to another conclusion which does help us with the Theatre: since the second Globe, according to a rent return of 1634, was built "upon an old foundation" which was of course that of the burnt-down first Globe,[24] it is clear that the frame of the second Globe was of the same diameter and shape of ground plan as that of the first; and therefore also of the same diameter and shape of ground plan as that of the Theatre. About the second Globe, thanks to Hollar, we know a great deal. Thus if we would like an impression of what, in general, the exterior of the Theatre looked like, we have only to glance at Hollar's depiction of the second Globe in the Long Bird's-Eye View of London or in the preliminary sketch for that engraving. Setting aside the hut of the second Globe (which was of an altogether different design from that of the Theatre hut), we may notice first Hollar's depiction of two three-story staircases attached to the frame of the playhouse; they have gabled roofs, the ridges of which connect with the ridge of the frame. Secondly we may notice Hollar's depiction of the second Globe as fully round; hence, unfortunately, the number of sides of the playhouse frame is not clear. And thirdly we may notice the height of the frame, for it permits us to make a good guess at the diameter of the frame. Hollar draws the playhouse frame of the second Globe about three times as wide as its height to the eaves, and that height, if we use the vertical dimensions given in the Fortune contract, may be estimated as about 33 feet 4 inches. Thus the diameter of the second Globe would have been about 100 feet; Hodges has estimated it as 92 feet;[25] I would estimate it as 96 feet.[26] We may conclude that the Theatre, like the first and second Globe after it, had a diameter of somewhere between 92 and 100 feet. It was a large playhouse.

So far in this essay I have attempted, where possible, to relate the Theatre to the tradition of later public playhouses about which we have some detailed knowledge. I should like now to relate the Theatre to the tradition of a well-documented earlier playhouse built in France more than fifty years before the Theatre by English workmen under the supervision of an English court administrator.

This is the banqueting house which King Henry VIII, in July 1520, immediately after the Field of the Cloth of Gold, caused to be built within the English city of Calais in order to entertain the Emperor Charles V with "some goodly mummery," a supper, a banquet, and "pastimes of dances and other disports as it shall stand with the King's pleasure." Responsibility for building the banqueting house was entrusted to Sir Edward Belknap, Knight of the Garter, who had overseen the construction of Henry's timber palace at the Castle of Guisnes and other buildings on the Field of the Cloth of Gold: "Item, as touching the making of the banquet house, the charge thereof is committed to Sir Edward Belknap." The "devising of the pageants at the banquet" was "committed" to William Cornish, Master of the King's Chapel.[27] Presumably these "pageants" were the eight masques mentioned by Hall.[28] The chief artists and craftsmen connected with the enterprise, all much experienced in the providing of court entertainments, were John Browne, Richard Gibson, John Rastell, and Clement

Urmeston; Sydney Anglo has a useful discussion of their achievements and of what they are known to have contributed to the Calais banqueting house.[29] The construction was presumably undertaken by some of the workmen brought to France by Belknap and two fellow-commissioners for the purpose of building Henry's timber palace at Guisnes and other works: according to Stow, "the King's Master Mason, Master Carpenter, and 300 masons, and 500 carpenters, 100 joiners, many painters, glaziers, tilers, smiths, and other artificers, both out of England and Flanders, to the number in all of 2,000 and more."[30] And the timber used in construction of the banqueting house may have been among that which Stow tells us was floated from England for Henry's "palace" at Guisnes.

One of our two chief sources of information about Henry's banqueting house is the account by Richard Turpin, "of Calais and burgess there," in his manuscript work, *The Chronicle of Calais*.[31] On July 11, Henry, having been entertained by Charles the day before in the imperial town of Gravelines, escorted the emperor to Calais, where the Emperor and his immediate retinue were lodged in the Staple Hall. Turpin continues:

> And [at] their coming there was made a banqueting house within the town of Calais, with sixteen principals made of great masts, betwixt every mast 24 foot; and all the outsides closed with board; and canvas over it. And within, round about by the sides, were made three lofts, one above another, for men and women for to stand upon; and they that stood behind might see over the heads that stood before, it was made so high behind and low before. And in the midst of the same banqueting house was set up a great piece [i.e., contrivance] of timber, made of eight great masts and bound together with great ropes and iron bands for to hold the masts together, for it was an 134 foot of length and cost £6.13s.4d. to set it upright. And the banqueting house was covered over with canvas and fastened with ropes. And within the said house was painted the element[s], with[32] stars, sun, and moon, and clouds, with divers other things made above over men's heads. And

there was great images of white wickers, like great men, and they were set high above on the highest lofts and stages; . . . And about the high piece of timber that stood upright in the midst was made stages of timber for organs and other instruments for to stand in, and men for to play upon them, and for clerks singing, and other pageants for to be played when the Kings of England and of Romans should be at their banquet. But on the same morning the wind began to rise, and at night blew off all the canvas and all the elements, with the stars, sun, and moon, and clouds; and the same rain blew out above a thousand torches and tapers that were ordained for the same; and all the Kings' seats that was made with great riches that could be ordained, besides all other things, was all dashed and lost.

As a result of this disaster the entertainment had to be given indoors, in the relatively confined space of the Exchequer of Calais, which enforced a much smaller audience than had been intended. Within a few days both Charles and Henry left Calais, and the banqueting house was presumably pulled down without ever having been used. *Sic transit gloria regum*.

Our other chief source of information is the description by the Venetian secretary, Marino Sanuto,[33] who goes into even greater detail than Turpin.

On Thursday the 12th [of July], the King and Queen dined with the Emperor and Madame Margaret [Duchess of Savoy] at Staple Hall; and in the evening a great banquet was to have been given in an amphitheatre recently erected for this purpose by the King; but the canvas roof having been blown off by a heavy gale of wind, it became requisite to change the site, and the banquet was served in the King's house [the Exchequer], but confusedly, by reason of the narrow space; and also in a private manner, for there were only a few personages present, not even the ambassadors. As the design of this theatre was very handsome, it must be described.

In front of the King's house is a fine open space formed by the demolition of sundry buildings, on which spot they

constructed this edifice entirely of timber. It has sixteen
fronts [*faze*], and its height and diameter measure each
upwards of 250 feet. In the centre of the building is the tall
mast of a ship, supported by other masts, the mainmast
rising to a sufficient height above the walls for the formation of a handsome and well proportioned covering, like a
pavilion. Around the summit of the mainmast are two
iron hoops with rings, one hoop being lower than the
other, from which hoops ropes are drawn to the walls all
round, and thereon rests the canvas covering. Beneath the
uppermost hoop the ropes, drawn in like manner from the
lower one, support another sort of azure-coloured canvas,
which forms the ceiling, being decorated with gold stars
and planets of looking glass.

Around the walls below the ceiling are three tiers of
balconies or stages, 8 or 9 feet deep, the parapet in front
being of the height of a man's waist, and the tiers raised
10 feet one above the other, with sloping floors, so that the
last look over the first, and behold conveniently what is
passing on the ground floor.

These tiers are spacious, and intended for the convenience of the spectators, musicians, trumpeters, etc.

. . . The parapet of the balconies on which the spectators
leant was covered with white cloth, hanging over the
length of 2 yards, like tapestry, with a border of green ivy
all round; and in the centre of the field were large white
roses and gilt rosettes; each of the three tiers being decorated in like manner. From the ceiling there hung large
chandeliers at each angle of the theatre, and between every
two chandeliers there was a human figure in the air of
wicker-work, and covered and clad with silk or cloth, and
bearing torches in their hands, all in different costumes,
and of alternate sexes, man and woman. Below these lights
were cornucopias, with foliage, which likewise served for
candlesticks, being fixed on the masts.

Round the centre mast tables were placed, forming a
square, and which were to have been prepared for the sovereigns; and there were other tables all round for the
company.

Fronting the entrance of this banqueting hall steps had been raised for a very large sideboard. The approach to this hall was through a vestibule 30 feet long and upwards of 15 broad, and in front of its entry were three statues. . . .

In the vestibule were six gilt statues of kings, three on each side; and at the entrance, over the door of the theatre, there were also three statues, . . .

Within the theatre, at the entrance, were the "old" arms of England and the imperial eagle, being placed in like manner all around, together with the two swords.

In this place, and in the fashion described, the banquet was to have been made; but the westerly wind, hearing the report and fearing it might be too hot in so enclosed a place, stripped off the covering and ceiling; and, scattering the fire, the air, the sea, and the land, left the site for the spectators, I suppose, the ruin being so complete that for them alone was there any accommodation.

A third important source of information is the anonymous *Triomphe festif . . . fait . . . en la ville de Calais* (Arras, 1520). This I have not seen, but I have used two or three details quoted by Sydney Anglo.

Our three sources, all apparently providing eyewitness accounts, make it possible to reconstruct the Calais banqueting house in considerable detail. The reconstruction, here illustrated in a series of drawings by Dale Frens, is based on the following interpretations of the available evidence.

1. The banqueting house was a "round" building, being referred to by Sanuto as an "amphitheatre."[34]

2. The frame of the banqueting house, having "sixteen principals" (Turpin) or "sixteen fronts [*faze*]" (Sanuto), was built to a ground plan in the shape of a sixteen-sided polygon (Fig. 4).

3. According to Turpin the distance between each pair of principal posts of the frame was 24 feet. I interpret this dimension as measured between one exterior angle of the frame and the next; that is, as measured horizontally along an outer face of the frame between midpoints of the exposed outer surfaces of two successive round principal posts (Fig. 3). Thus the di-

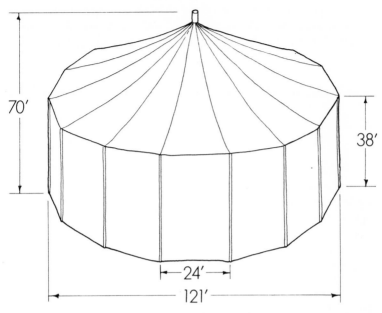

3. The Calais banqueting house.

ameter of the frame would have been 121 feet if measured from one side of the polygonal ground plan to the side opposite; or 123 feet if measured from the point of one angle of the polygon to that of the angle opposite. I believe that Turpin's method of indicating the size of the frame should inspire confidence, because the width of the face of a polygonal building can be measured relatively easily and accurately, whereas the diameter of such a building can usually be measured only with some difficulty and then rarely with much accuracy; for which reason the diameter given in a nontechnical description of such a building is usually based not on a measurement but on an estimate. In any case, the diameter of 121 or 123 feet indicated by Turpin's measurement of a side of the frame of the Calais banqueting house is pretty exactly corroborated by the statement, given in Sanuto's Italian text,[35] that the diameter of the building is "more than 50 paces"—that is, over 125 feet, the standard value of a single-step "pace" being about 2½ feet (*O.E.D.*, sb.[1], sense 3). Sanuto says also, in the long description

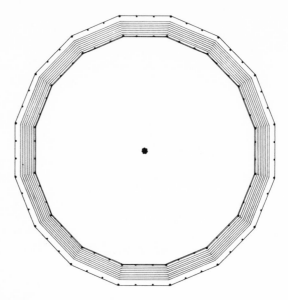

4. A plan of the first gallery of the Calais banqueting house.

quoted above, that the diameter of the building measures "upwards of 250 feet"—a statement which at first glance seems
incomprehensible but which correlates closely with the other
evidence cited if we suppose that it resulted from the misinter-
pretation of 50 single-step paces as 50 double-step paces, the
word "pace" in this alternative sense having of course the
value of about 5 feet. Thus Sanuto would again be giving the
diameter as over 125 feet. Finally, the author of the *Triomphe
festif* says that the banqueting house was 60 to 80 feet in
diameter.[36] This dimension (obviously an uncertain estimate)
is so widely divergent from those afforded by other evidence as
to suggest that it may relate not to the diameter but to the
radius of the building. If so, the diameter indicated would be
120 to 160 feet, a range that includes the dimension of 121 or
123 feet implied by Turpin's statement and Sanuto's dimension of over 125 feet.[37]

4. The frame of the banqueting house had three stories (Fig.
5), variously called "lofts" and "stages" (Turpin), "balconies or

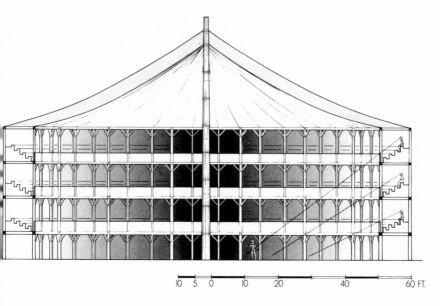

5. A section of the Calais banqueting house.

stages" (Sanuto), and "galeries" (*Le Triomphe festif*).[38] All three accounts explain that the galleries were superimposed one over another. Sanuto says that each story was 10 feet high. I interpret this dimension as from floor to floor; thus the height of the three galleries would have measured 30 feet from the floor of the first to the top of the third gallery.

5. In the reconstruction I have set the floor of the first gallery at an elevation of 8 feet above ground level (Fig. 5), in accordance with the style recorded in contemporary illustrations depicting scaffolds or galleries for spectators at tournaments. Thus there would have been, directly beneath the first story of the frame, an open space some 9 feet deep and some 7 feet high in the clear—a sort of ground story except that it would have lacked the floor and structural underpinnings usually connoted by the term "story." The height of the frame, from ground level to the top of the third gallery, would thus have been 38 feet.

6. The principal posts of the frame, since characterized by

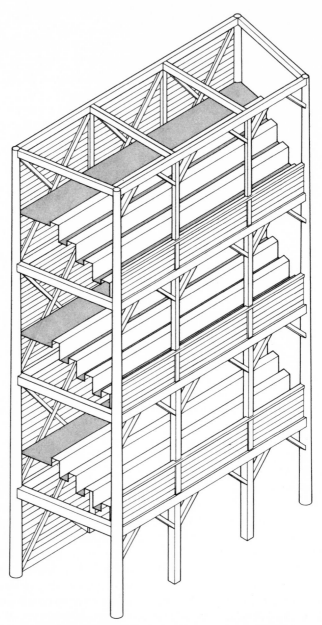

6. One of the sixteen bays of the frame of the Calais
banqueting house.

Turpin as "masts" (*O.E.D.*, sb.[1], sense 1b), would have been round timbers (about the diameter of a modern telephone pole) extending the full height of the frame (38 feet). (See Fig. 6.) Since the principal posts presumably extended some 5 feet below ground level, the total length of the timbers used may be imagined as about 43 feet. In the reconstruction I have made the principal posts about 11 inches in diameter at mid-point of the ground "story," the posts progressively diminishing to about 10, 9, and 8 inches in diameter at midpoints of, respectively, the first, second, and third stories of the frame. Moreover, since both the 24-foot span between principals of the outer face of the frame and the 20-foot span between principals of the inner face (see following paragraph) would have needed support, I have supposed two prick-posts standing between each pair of principal posts in both the outer and inner faces of the frame, the four posts in question standing at intervals (on centres) of 8 feet in the outer face, of 6, 8, and 6 feet respectively in the inner. I have imagined the prick-posts as dimensioned timbers measuring 8, 7, 6 and 5 inches square in ascending order of the stories of the frame.

7. According to Sanuto the galleries were "8 or 9 feet deep." Interpreting this as an internal measurement, I have given the depth of the frame as 9 feet 11 inches measured from the extreme front to the extreme rear of the frame at mid-elevation of the ground "story" (Fig. 5); thus the length of an inner face of the frame would have been 20 feet (Fig. 4). Since the principal posts narrowed toward the top of the frame, the depth of frame as measured "from outside to outside" diminishes slightly in the three upper stories, to a depth of 9 feet 8 inches at mid-elevation of the top story of the frame. And since the prick-posts, diminishing in size toward the top of the frame, were presumably centred on the tapered principal posts, the internal dimension of the depths of the galleries increases slightly as the structure rises: it is 8 feet 5 inches in the first gallery, increasing to 8 feet 6 inches in the second and to 8 feet 7 inches in the third—all dimensions in the clear between prick-posts of the outer and inner walls of the frame (3 inches less between corresponding outer and inner principal posts). Thus the depths of the three galleries, as reconstructed, strike a

mean (8 feet 6 inches) corresponding to the mean value of Sanuto's dimension "8 or 9 feet."

8. In the reconstruction I have supposed cross-bracing in the outer wall of the frame, angle bracing in the inner (Fig. 6).

9. Both Turpin and Sanuto indicate that the gallery standings or seats were stepped for the accommodation of spectators' sightlines. I have assumed four rows of seats in each gallery, rising by steps of 9 inches in the first gallery, 11 inches in the second, and 13 inches in the third; a seat-height of 18 inches throughout; and a 20-inch depth of seating throughout (Figs. 5, 6). Thus there would have been, at the back of each gallery, a raised access passageway some 2 feet wide (in the clear of the prick-posts) running completely round the frame (Figs. 4, 6).

10. The gallery-fronts ("parapets") were as high as a man's waist (Sanuto). I have interpreted this as 3 feet in the first gallery, 2 feet 10 inches in the second, and 2 feet 8 inches in the third.

11. According to Turpin the outer walls of the frame were covered with a sheathing of boards ("all the outsides closed with board"). I have assumed that the sheathing was applied to the outside of the outer wall of the frame (Fig. 6); but it might conceivably have been applied to the inside of the outer wall.

12. Turpin says that in the centre of the banqueting house there stood "a great piece of timber, made of eight great masts and bound together with great ropes and iron bands"—a sort of giant *fasces* (Fig. 5). He here uses the word *piece* in the sense of "piece of work" or "contrivance" (*O.E.D.*, sense 17a, *Obs.*). (Stow, copying Turpin in his *Chronicles*, changes "piece of timber" to "pillar of timber.") Sanuto calls this pieced-together column, at first mention, "the tall mast of a ship, supported by other masts"; thereafter, "the mainmast" or "the centre mast." Turpin gives the height of the column as 134 feet, Sanuto as 250; neither dimension (even if Sanuto's 250 feet be an error for 125) is practicable. Fortunately, Sanuto's description suggests something more modest: the mainmast, he says, rose "to a sufficient height above the walls for the formation of a handsome and well proportioned covering, like a pavil-

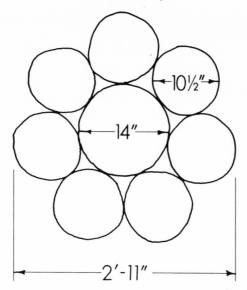

7. A cross-section at ground level of the central
column of the Calais banqueting house.

ion." I have therefore assumed a central column rising 70 feet
above ground level and, for the sake of stability, extending
some 10 feet below ground. Since the number of masts composing the column was eight, the core mast must have been of
greater diameter than the seven masts of the surrounding ring.
I have supposed a core mast about 14 inches in diameter at
ground level, surrounded by seven supporting masts each
about 10½ inches in diameter at ground level (Fig. 7). Thus the
diameter of the column would have been about 2 feet 11 inches
at ground level; presumably it tapered to a diameter of about
1 foot 9 inches at the top. I have supposed that the masts were
bound together by "great ropes" (Turpin) at approximately
8-foot intervals; thus the several individual masts composing
the column could each have consisted of two or three timbers
placed end to end, the joins of two-part masts being staggered
in relation to those of adjacent three-part masts so as to ensure
the rigidity of the whole column (Fig. 5). Because the length of
the column was greater than the radius of the arena, it must
have been erected before the surrounding frame of the banquet-

ing house, being temporarily guyed to stakes near the perimeter of the arena until after erection of the frame.

13. Near the top of the central column, according to Sanuto, were "two iron hoops with rings, one hoop being lower than the other, from which hoops ropes are drawn to the walls all around" (Fig. 5). (Presumably Sanuto's "iron hoops" correspond to Turpin's "iron bands.") The ropes "drawn to the walls all around" appear to have had two functions: to serve as guy-lines to help stabilize the long and massive central column, and to support a double canvas covering of the banqueting house. The ropes of an upper system, attached to rings of the upper hoop, were drawn, presumably, to the top of the outer wall of the frame so as to support an upper canvas cover which served as a roof; and the ropes of a lower system, attached to rings of the lower hoop, were drawn, presumably, to the top of the inner wall of the frame so as to support a lower canvas cover which served as a ceiling.[39] Thus the third story of the frame, unless it had its own canvas ceiling, would have been covered only by the upper canvas cover serving as roof of the whole. I assume that each canvas cover was supported by a system of forty-eight ropes, each of the ropes being connected with the top of the frame (whether the outer or the inner wall) at a point directly above a principal post or a prick-post. Thus the central column would have been guyed to the frame of the banqueting house by a double system consisting of ninety-six lines.

14. On the canvas ceiling was painted an enormous cosmological *mappa mundi* showing aspects of the four elements including the planets; this is described briefly by Turpin and at some length by Sanuto in passages omitted from the quotations given above. Anglo provides an enlightening discussion of this ceiling painting and other features of the decoration of the banqueting house (pp. 160–63).

15. Turpin tells us that "stages of timber" were placed round the central column, "for organs and other instruments to stand in, and men for to play upon them, and for clerks singing, and other pageants for to be played." Sanuto says that "tables . . . forming a square" were placed round the central

column for the sovereigns, and that "there were other tables all round for the company." Because of the uncertainties involved I have not ventured upon a reconstruction of the stages and tables.

16. The entrance to the banqueting house was through a "vestibule" 30 feet long and more than 15 feet wide (Sanuto). Since neither the height nor the design of this vestibule is known, I have not attempted to show it in the drawings. The entranceway proper to the arena of the banqueting house would of course have been through one of the 7-foot-high bays of the ground "story" of the frame.

17. No information is available on the means of access to the galleries. Presumably it was by an external staircase or staircases, perhaps comparable (*mutatis mutandis*) to the timber staircase depicted in the Great Tournament Roll of Westminster of 1501.[40]

18. There is also no information regarding the surface of the arena, which may well have consisted of the original earth, levelled, raked, and compacted. On the other hand, the arena may have been covered with a wooden floor, as in the case of a comparable structure at Paris in 1518 (see note 41 below).

Although there are some uncertainties about the Calais banqueting house, the general character of its design is clear. Its existence suggests, more than fifty years before construction of Burbage's Theatre, an English tradition of playhouse design capable of producing a "round" three-story timber building measuring 121 feet in diameter, built to a ground plan in the shape of a sixteen-sided polygon, and having stepped standings or seats within its three galleries for the better accommodation of spectators' sightlines.[41] This generalized description is fairly close to our understanding of the Elizabethan and Jacobean tradition of public-playhouse design based on such sources as the Swan drawing, the Fortune and Hope contracts, and Hollar's Long Bird's-Eye View of London. Apparently the Theatre, despite such differences as being smaller than the Calais banqueting house, lacking a central column supporting a canvas roof and ceiling, having a superstructure hut, and having also a single stage standing in front of a tiring-house somehow integrated with the surrounding playhouse frame, was not, in the essential features of its design, a new thing under the sun in 1576.

Notes

1. W. W. Braines, *Holywell Priory and the Site of the Theatre, Shoreditch* (London, 1923). Throughout the present essay I have generally modernized the spelling and punctuation of Renaissance texts and titles. I have also made some minor editorial changes in quoting from modern sources.
2. E. K. Chambers, *The Elizabethan Stage* (Oxford, 1923), II, 362, 358; IV, 200; II, 5; IV, 197, 223. In translating Kiechel's now archaic Middle High German word *ettwann* as "in some instances" I assume the basic etymological sense of "sometimes" or "occasionally." Chambers, who translates it as "about," apparently mistook the word for New High German *etwa*, "approximately." (Kluge, *Etymologisches Wörterbuch*.)
3. C. W. Wallace, *The First London Theatre* (Lincoln, Nebr., 1913), pp. 152, 105.
4. Ibid., p. 178; Chambers, II, 467, 437.
5. Wallace, pp. 114, 112; Chambers, II, 466. The appropriate detail of Hollar's engraving is reproduced by C. Walter Hodges in *The Globe Restored*, rev. ed. (London, 1968), Plate 4. In Plate 5 Hodges reproduces also Hollar's preliminary sketch for the Long View entitled "The West Part of Southwark toward Westminster," which shows the second Globe and the Hope from approximately the same point of view as in the engraving.
6. Wallace, p. 126; reproduction of the Swan Drawing in Hodges, Plate 3.
7. Wallace, p. 127.
8. This assumption is confirmed by evidence of the five extant plays which, because their generally accepted dates of composition fall within the period when the Chamberlain's Men were playing at the Theatre (from 1594 to early 1597), we may suppose to have been designed for original production at the Theatre: Shakespeare's *Richard II*, *Romeo and Juliet*, *A Midsummer Night's Dream*, *The Merchant of Venice*, and *King John*. These tell us that the tiring-house of the Theatre had (1) two doors to the stage suitable for entrances "at several doors"; (2) a small curtained "discovery-space" suitable for the discovery of Portia's three caskets or of the recumbent Juliet as in a "tomb"; and (3) a shallow "upper station" suitable for the appearance of

Jessica or of Romeo and Juliet as at the upper-story window of a house, of Prince Arthur or of Richard II and four other actors as upon the walls of a castle, or of the Citizen of Angiers as upon the walls of that city. Thus the discovery-space of the Theatre could have been the doorway of a 6- or 7-foot-wide door like one of those shown in the Swan drawing, the double-hung leaves of the door having been opened out through 180 degrees and laid flat against the tiring-house façade and the open doorway having been fitted up with curtains or hangings; and the upper station of the Theatre could have been a shallow space immediately behind the 6-foot-wide window of a box like one of those depicted by De Witt in the upper story of the Swan tiring-house.

9. See D. F. Rowan, "A Neglected Jones/Webb Theatre Project," *Shakespeare Survey 23* (1970), pp. 125–29 and Plates I-II. John Orrell, in "Inigo Jones at the Cockpit" (*Shakespeare Survey 30* [1977], pp.·157–68 and Plates II-V), makes the attractive suggestion that the playhouse in question is the Cockpit or Phoenix.

10. Chambers, II, 436–37; J. Q. Adams, *Shakespearean Playhouses* (Boston, 1917), p. 48n.

11. "'This Wooden O'," *The Times* (London), March 26, 1954, p. 7. On p. 14 Hotson reproduces the left half of the Utrecht view, showing the sweep of the city and its northern suburbs from St. Paul's Church to Shoreditch. Hotson repeats his arguments in *Shakespeare's Wooden O* (London, 1959), pp. 304–13.

12. *The Theatre, the Curtain, and the Globe* (Montreal: McGill University Library, 1964). More recently, Fisher has given additional information about the techniques of establishing an artist's point of view and computing the bearings of depicted buildings, in an unpublished paper presented at a meeting of the Theatre History Seminar of the Shakespeare Association of America chaired by D. F. Rowan (Toronto, 1978).

13. Fisher, p. 3.

14. Ibid., p. 4.

15. There is also a third, relatively little used, convention in which the polygonal building is represented as fully round but as having also the corners which resulted from the interfacing of each pair of contiguous sides; thus the represented building gives the appearance of having curved "sides." An example is afforded by the so-called Agas view of London (c. 1633), in which two of the Bankside animal-baiting houses of the 1560s are shown as fully round buildings each having about twenty curved "sides"; and another by the Faithorne and Newcourt view of London (1658), in which the Hope is represented as a fully round building having about sixteen curved "sides" (but about twenty-seven roof bays). This convention is used also, with adaptation appropriate to the difference between a plan and a view, in the Paris Garden

Manor Map (1627), in which the Swan is represented as a fully round building divided into fifteen bays, hence having fifteen curved "sides."

16. Richard Hosley, "The Swan Playhouse," in *The Revels History of Drama in English*, III, *1576–1613* (London, 1975), pp. 144–48 and Figs. 11–13. Compare also the fifteen-sided representation reproduced as Fig. 10.

17. A literal interpretation of the roof line of the fully depicted playhouse of the Utrecht view is made by Rosemary Linnell in her reconstruction of the Curtain as an eight-sided playhouse measuring 26½ feet in diameter from face to face: *The Curtain Playhouse* (London, 1977), p. 46.

18. So Hodges, p. 110.

19. At least in the 1590s, the general date of the Utrecht view. Elsewhere in the present volume Professor Wickham suggests that the Theatre may not have had a hut until after about 1590.

20. A cupola is shown as surmounting the superstructure hut of the first Globe in the Visscher view of London (1616); and a cupola or lantern as surmounting the hut of the second Globe both in Hollar's Long Bird's-Eye View of London (1647) and in the Merian View of London (1638).

21. Wallace, pp. 277–79; Chambers, II, 399, 417. The length of time required to dismantle the Theatre is uncertain. Professor Berry, elsewhere in the present volume, suggests that the job took from two to four days. C. C. Stopes, in "The Burbages and the Transportation of the Theatre" (*Athenaeum*, October 16, 1909), suggests that the timbers of the Theatre may have been carried across the Thames by water in order to avoid wheelage and passage dues on London Bridge. C. Walter Hodges has a charming fictional account of the dismantling of the Theatre and the transportation of its timbers in *Playhouse Tales* (London, 1974). The timbers of the Theatre are heard of at least once again before being destroyed by fire in 1613. Though they seem ultimately to have given good service for thirty-seven years, in 1600 they were judged to be not so heavy as they might have been, for the Fortune contract requires that the builder of that playhouse (Peter Street) "make all the said frame in every point for scantlings larger and bigger in assize than the scantlings of the timber of the said new erected house called the Globe" (Chambers, II, 438).

22. Chambers, II, 415.

23. "Theatre into Globe," *Shakespeare Quarterly* III (1952), no. 2: 113–20. Smith prints useful drawings of various kinds of joints and carpenter's marks.

24. Chambers, II, 426.

25. *Shakespeare's Second Globe* (London, 1973).

26. A diameter of some such magnitude would presumably have been

necessary in a playhouse large enough to accommodate an audience of more than 3,000 spectators—the capacity of the second Globe as recorded by the Spanish ambassador in 1624 in his official reports of the popular success of Middleton's violently anti-Spanish play *A Game at Chess*: "The actors whom they call here 'the King's Men' have recently acted, and are still acting, in London a play that so many people come to see, that there were more than 3,000 persons there on the day that the audience was smallest." And again: "It cannot be pleaded that those who repeat and hear these insults are merely four rogues because during these last four days more than 12,000 persons have all heard the play of *A Game at Chess*, for so they call it, including all the nobility still in London." Quotations from G. E. Bentley, *The Jacobean and Caroline Stage*, VI *Theatres* (Oxford, 1968), p. 184. According to De Witt, the Swan also had a capacity of 3,000 (Chambers, II, 362).

27. *Rutland Papers*, ed. W. J. Jerdan (London: Camden Society, 1842), pp. 54–56.

28. *The Union of the Two Noble and Illustre Families of Lancaster and York* (1548), sig. OOo6ᵛ: "Tuesday [i.e., Thursday] the 12th day of July, because the banquet house could not be finished, the Emperor and the Lady Margaret supped with the King and the Queen at the Checker, where the same night after supper revelled ninety-six maskers; after the revels was a banquet.... This night was eight companies of maskers, and in every company twelve persons, all in gold, silver, and velvet richly apparelled; but because the room was small the show was the less."

29. *Spectacle, Pageantry, and Early Tudor Policy* (Oxford, 1969), pp. 164–68.

30. *The Chronicles of England* (1580), p. 924.

31. Ed. J. G. Nichols (London: Camden Society, 1846), pp. 29–30. The extant manuscript (British Library, MS. Harl. 542) is a transcript by Stow, who printed an excerpt relating to the banqueting house in his *Chronicles* (1580), pp. 927–28. Stow's account of the banqueting house was reprinted in the second edition of Holinshed's *Chronicles* (1587).

32. For "with" (MS. "wᵗʰ") Nichols misprints "of". I am indebted to Professor Roger Dahood for checking the text here quoted from Nichols against that of the Stow transcript in the British Library.

33. *Calendar of State Papers, Venice, 1520–26*, pp. 32–34, translating from Sanuto's Diaries.

34. Compare the "rotunda" erected by Francis I at Ardres in June 1520: a banqueting house whose cloth roof was supported by "tall masts lashed together to increase their length" (ibid., p. 42; Anglo, pp. 140–41).

35. Anglo, p. 159n, quoting from Sanuto's *Diarii*, ed. F. Stefani (Venice, 1879–1902): "il diametro è più di cinquanta passa."
36. Anglo, p. 159.
37. The English chronicles, which have negligible or no authority in the matter, betray some confusion about the size of the banqueting house. Hall (1548) says that it was "80 foot round." Presumably he meant "80 feet in radius" (cf. *O.E.D.*, round, *adv.* and *prep.*, sense 3b: "By measurement in all directions from a given centre"). This gives a diameter of 160 feet—a fairly large figure but perhaps not an obviously improbable one. Stow (1580), using Hall as well as Turpin, seems to have been unhappy with Hall's "80 foot round," which he presumably understood in the sense of "80 feet in circumference" (cf. *O.E.D.*, round, *adj.*, sense 4d: "Of measure: Circumferential"). Since this yields the clearly impossible diameter of about 25½ feet, Stow apparently changed Hall's dimension to "800 foot compass" (i.e., circumference). This yields a diameter of about 255 feet, which is also clearly impossible but was nevertheless accepted by Holinshed (1587).
38. Anglo, p. 160.
39. Two canvas covers were used as roof and ceiling of the disguising house built by Henry viii at Greenwich in 1527; see Anglo, pp. 215 ff.
40. *The Great Tournament Roll of Westminster*, ed. Sydney Anglo (Oxford, 1968), m. 34.
41. I have called this postulated tradition English because the Calais banqueting house, although sited on what had been and was again to be French soil, was designed by English court officials and built by English workmen in a then English city for the entertainment of an English court by English artists, musicians, and maskers. The tradition may have been influenced by a French tradition represented by the banqueting house built by Francis i in Paris in 1518 for the reception of English ambassadors; but our present state of knowledge makes it difficult to say in what ways or to what extent such an influence may have operated. For information about the Paris banqueting house of 1518 we are again indebted to Marino Sanuto: "On December 22nd the banquet was held in the Bastille, a small fortress. In its centre was a large space, which was floored with timber, and three galleries were erected all round, one above the other, the whole being covered in with an awning of blue canvas well waxed and powdered with gilt stars, signs, and planets. . . . A large platform, on which the benches were placed; . . . At the end of the platform was a dais of cloth of gold, . . . On the floor below the platform were two tables filled inside and out with the gentlemen of the English embassy and many French gentlemen, with ladies. . . . After supper several companies of

masquers appeared. . . . The Queen and Madame Louise viewed the sight from one of the galleries." Some additional details are furnished by the author of another account: "In the courtyard a very handsome temporary building had been erected; the floor was planked and carpeted. . . . Three tiers of balconies for the spectators. At one end was a platform about 10 yards wide, with a row of columns. . . . Dais of cloth of gold for the King and the English ambassadors. . . . At the close of the repast the tables were noiselessly removed, and those who did not dance went aloft into the galleries." (*C. S. P., Ven., 1520–26*, pp. 485–86.) The evidence does not, unfortunately, indicate whether the Paris banqueting house was built to a round or a rectangular ground plan. However, another example of the French tradition, Francis I's banqueting house at Ardres in 1520, was a round building (see note 34 above).

Why Didn't Burbage Lease the Beargarden?
A Conjecture in Comparative Architecture

Oscar Brownstein

"In 1576 when James Burbage came to build a permanent home for his company he chose a site outside the limits of the City of London, in Shoreditch, where he and what was now the Lord Chamberlain's company could perform free from ever-increasing restrictions of the City authorities. Here he built the Theatre in the open fields. This was an unroofed theatre whose form was adapted from the bull and bear baiting yards sometimes used as suitable enclosures by the players."[1]

The quotation is from Richard Leacroft's recent book. Except for the blunders about the name of Burbage's company in 1576 and the "open fields," there is nothing remarkable in the passage: its attitudes, assumptions, and hypotheses are in the public domain. Leacroft cites no supporting evidence or authority for his statements, which he offers abundantly elsewhere but that merely points up his certainty that he is asserting widely accepted facts.

What evidence has he that Burbage adopted the form of the bull- and bear-baiting yards or that players had previously performed in such places? The primary document was published in 1953 by C. W. Hodges; it is a drawing of players setting up a stage within a circular Swan-like auditorium which is called a baiting arena.[2] Of course, the drawing is in Hodges's own hand and from his own head, but it has had no less evidential effect for that; it condenses in black and white a visualization of what oft was thought but ne'er so concretely imagined.

I will not cite the historians who have alluded to or built theories on the alleged seminal relationship of the baiting arena or so-called gamehouse to the design of the Theatre— they are well-known. But I think this notion is worth questioning, and I want to question it in a small way by means of a counterfactual conditional: if the baiting arenas were so readily adaptable for stage-plays, why didn't Burbage merely lease a beargarden?

There is no obvious commercial reason why Burbage did not lease or convert one of the baiting places on the Bankside. He would almost certainly have reduced the amount of his investment—which seems to have come to £200 of his own money—and he would not have had to tie himself to a partnership with his brother-in-law. Presumably there would have been no change in the usual routine of the players setting up in a beargarden, no added inconveniences to those normally met on tour—fewer, indeed, because this would be a permanent or at least extended residency. The company would have been no further from the population centres than was Holywell. The Bankside was a far better-known location and one more commonly associated with popular entertainments; moreover, the Liberty of the Clink seems to have been at least as well protected from civic interference as Holywell. If crossing the river was a liability to the site, it could not have been much of one. I think we must quite rule out the location of the baiting arenas as a *deterrent* to Burbage, for that is just where that shrewd investor, Philip Henslowe, built his Rose playhouse ten years later—and, perhaps, with greater immediate success than Burbage—and, of course, that is just where Burbage's sons moved his theatre building.

Nor does there seem to have been an impediment because of the lack of availability of baiting rings. In the thirty .years between 1546 and 1576 there were no fewer than six—perhaps more—short-lived baiting places on the Bankside; most of these were very simple, and probably no more than two of them existed at any time, but in 1575 the two most elaborate and durable baiting places yet constructed were not only still standing, but available.[3] One of these, built by William Payne, is reported to have had standings; this baiting arena was to evolve into the Beargarden and, subsequently, into the Hope. The other baiting place was built and operated by Robert Wistowe until 1575 when he purchased the lease of Payne's arena from Payne's widow and transferred his operations to that baiting place.[4] There is no record that Wistowe's former baiting ring was used for baiting again, and a few years later the property was converted to other uses; but in 1575 it was standing idle, ready to hand for Burbage to lease or purchase if it was a suitable enclosure for players. Or, if Wistowe's old ring was somehow uniquely unsuitable, there is no reason to rule out a part-time lease of Wistowe's new ring. Baitings were conducted only on Sundays and holidays, in this period,[5] and though these were probably the players' best days, the players were then playing daily and would give up Sundays only four years later without any crippling effect.[6] In the 1590s Henslowe would be using the Rose for plays six days a week and the Beargarden for baitings on Sundays;[7] if the Beargarden was adaptable for plays, one wonders why he used two different buildings, one for plays and the other for baitings. He must have wondered about that, too. Perhaps that it why he built the Hope to replace both and thereby reduce the cost of upkeep by half.

Thus, if Hodges, Leacroft, and others were correct about the usefulness of the baiting arenas to the players, then Burbage—not to mention Henslowe—was a far less astute businessman than we had thought, for at least two well-developed baiting places were available, one for lease or sublease and one, probably the less elaborately developed of the two, for purchase. Of course, there may have been special personal conditions influencing Burbage which we don't know, but then why didn't someone else take up so obvious and so inexpensive an opportunity? There is neither evidence nor substantial grounds

for conjecture that *any* public playhouse was converted from
a baiting ring, temporarily or permanently, as were the innyards. There is no record of an old baiting place in the vicinity
of the Theatre or Curtain, much less previously on those sites
and, though there is evidence of an old baiting site near the
Rose, long since out of use, the Rose was not built on that
site.[8] In the nineteenth century some theatre historians be-
lieved the Swan to be a converted baiting arena or at least a
convertible, multi-use amphitheatre, but no evidence has been
found to support this notion. It arose because Elizabethans
sometimes called the Beargarden the Paris Garden, and the
Swan (unlike the Beargarden) was in the Manor of Paris
Garden.[9]

So why didn't Burbage or Henslowe or Langley or anybody
else lease or purchase an unused baiting arena instead of building a playhouse? It wasn't because the baiting arenas were
badly located, or unavailable, or too expensive, surely. Despite
apparent similarities between the baiting arenas and the playhouses, at least in their circular plans, is it possible that these
buildings were so different in design that they could not be
easily employed interchangeably? There is both a kind of general and some quite specific evidence which suggests just that.
The hypothesis I wish to pursue is that playhouses and baiting
arenas accommodated their audiences in such different ways,
consistent with their different histories and functions, that
they had little in common.

To begin with, we must make a distinction between bull- and
bear-baiting; though by the sixteenth century they were joined
in the royal and in the commercial baiting establishments,
they had developed separately.[10] Bull- and bear-baiting had
different purposes, different sponsors, different canine antago-
nists, and, more to our immediate point, different basic structural requirements. The fundamental structure for bull-baitings was the bull ring, a circular barrier from 20 to 30 feet
in diameter; it seems that virtually every market town in
England had one near its butcher's row in compliance with the
municipal laws requiring that butchers bait their bulls before
slaughter in order to render their bull beef non-toxic. The
barrier had to be large enough in circumference to permit the

bull to charge, and high and sturdy enough to keep the bull in and any spectators out. A loose bull in town, especially when chased by dogs, was a dangerous and destructive force.

The situation for bear-baitings was quite different. Baitings were conducted for private rather than public purposes, to aid in the breeding, training, and testing of the English mastiff, and, eventually, for competitive wagering upon him. Both the bears and the dogs were valuable properties not available to the lower classes. Bear-baiting began at the great manors in the Middle Ages, probably conducted in courtyards or tiltyards as records indicate they were in the sixteenth century; but when —records begin in the last quarter of the fifteenth century— the liveried bearwards began to take their bears around the countryside to permit local gentry to try their dogs in competition with others, the mode of presentation was a stake driven into the ground of an open field and the bear attached to the stake by a short rope or chain. The bear would circle the stake, rear up on its haunches to protect its neck and head and to strike with its forepaws, and then move again. The greatest danger at these open baitings was probably from wounded dogs, which were trained man-killers. If a bear did go berserk, and this seems to have happened sometimes, especially with bears which had been blinded through years of baitings, no mere bull ring would provide protection.

For either form of baiting the first and continuing concern was safety; the railed ring for the one and the stake for the other were the earliest physical accommodations for the spectator. The next physical development seems related to the desire to combine bull- and bear-baiting in the same arenas in London, and to a need to provide a greater, and perhaps more explicit, degree of safety. At some time in the first half of the sixteenth century—the earliest evidence dates from 1546[11] —the Yeoman of the King's Game began to conduct public baitings with the King's Bears and Apes in the fields in Southwark near the royal game park in Paris Garden.

The Braun and Hogenberg map view of London shows us two baiting rings in Southwark, labelled the bull-baiting and bear-baiting (see Fig. 1).[12] Though this has not been done by anyone so far as I can tell, these drawings *can* be taken as

1. "The Beare bayting," enlarged and redrawn (the origi-
nal is ¼-inch wide), from the engraving, "Londinum
Feracissimi Angliae Regni Metropolis," in Braun and
Hogenberg's *Civitates Orbis Terrarum* (1573), I.

relatively accurate and relatively well-drafted representations.
Depicted are two cylindrical constructions which seem to be
composed of heavy upright posts and circular top beams with
a lathed waist-high wall below; baitings are shown within,
spectators without. Both seem to be straightforward elabora-
tions of the bull ring, open cages composed of posts and beams
raised high enough to block dogs thrown by the bulls, to stop
the bull's charge, and to contain or at least slow the escape
of a bear that had broken from the stake.

There is independent pictorial corroboration for the essential
details of this literal interpretation in a crude manuscript
drawing by William Smith, a resident of London from about
1568 to about 1575. What he shows are two high circular

2. The bear-baiting ring, enlarged and redrawn (the original is ½-inch wide), from the coloured manuscript drawing, "London," in William Smith's *A Particular Description of England* (1588). See note.

corral-like structures (see Fig. 2); they are depicted from a raised point of view which would permit Smith to show easily any roofs, seats, or dimension to the enclosure walls. He does not.

In about 1600 William Faunte, knight and gamester, wrote to the proprietors of the Beargarden (by then a three-level amphitheatre) that his one-eyed bull, Bevis, would "ether throo vp your dodges in the loftes, or eles ding out theare braynes agenst the grates."[13] "Loft" must refer to the upper gallery, and it seems quite likely that "grate" refers to the enclosure of posts and beams shown in the map-views. This evidence suggests that the baiting ring was barred about with a grate eight to ten feet high, from William Payne's original enclosure through his addition of low standings and Wistowe's of an upper level, the rebuilding of the Beargarden in 1583 with two upper levels, until the Hope replaced the Beargarden in 1613.

If this is so, we can understand a number of apparent anomalies in the early descriptions of the baiting arenas. For instance, when "the stage at Paris Garden fell down all at ones" (as John Dee describes it) in 1583, all accounts agree that it was the spectators standing in the "yard" who suffered most injuries and fatalities. John Field says that the extraordinarily large crowd in attendance that day filled "the yeard, standings and Galleries." It is simply not credible that spectators would be permitted to share an undivided space with the baitings; therefore something like the grate would have to be inferred to explain the references to the spectators in the yard. Lambarde's simile in 1576, generalizing the segregation of the audience at the innyards and the Beargarden, makes sense only if there were standing space on the ground at the Beargarden to justify the fee difference between those who paid to enter at the gate and those who paid again to enter "the Scaffolde." Again, either the spectator is unprotected or we must infer a gratelike barrier. In his account of a visit to a commercial baiting in 1562, Allessandro Magno describes the place as "an open circular space surrounded by stands" and that "to enter below one pays one penny and two to go up into the stands": again the distinction between those in the stands and those on the ground. Magno says that the baiting ring itself "is closed about and there is no way out unless they open certain doors"[14]—an enclosure that prevented the escape of the animals and yet did not impede the vision of those standing on the ground could only have been the grate.

After the stake, the grate is the simplest and least expensive way to provide for the safety of audiences attending commercial baitings. Each of the four regular features of a commercial baiting had its attendant dangers: the bear-baitings presented potential hazards from the bear, should one get loose, and from wounded mastiffs; bull-baitings produced the certainty that dogs would be thrown upward and outward; whipping the blind bear was often conducted without a stake and chain, and a tormented blind bear was more dangerous to humans than the bear that could see; and baiting a chimpanzee on horse-back, the jackanapes, brought leaping hounds and a terrified horse to the outer circuit of the arena. The stake and chain for bear-baiting, the ring for bull-baiting, and the grate for the combination of baiting sports were the earliest physical devel-opments for baitings, and they were designed to protect rather than to enlarge the audience.

The stands mentioned by Magno, Lambarde, and Field are also of interest. The arena Magno visited must have been that then belonging to William Payne, because his is the only arena known to have "low scaffolds or standings" before the time of his death in 1574 or 1575;[15] it was probably the only one with them.[16] The "low standings" would not be possible were it not for an effectively transparent and yet safe barrier between them and the baitings.

In the playhouse the lowest level for the audience around the yard was a gallery for spectators; the galleries shown in the Swan drawing seem to be raised high enough to put the heads of seated spectators above the level of the stage. In the Bear-garden, on the other hand, the evidence suggests that the low-est scaffolding for spectators remained "low standings," such as Payne first built around the grate, until the Hope was erected. In other words, the lowest of the raised levels for spectators in the theatres and in the Beargarden seem to have quite different, the latter being both lower and for standing only (see Fig. 3).

These features of the early Beargarden—a grate surrounded by ground stands—produce a model of a special purpose arena which would be vastly inconvenient for the viewing of plays. Put a stage within this space and the results are distressing. Spectators standing in the yard will be divided into an inner and an outer ring, and those standing in the outer ring, on the ground as well as in the stands, must watch the performance on the stage through the grate. Plays were relatively inactive, verbal, and of long duration; baitings consisted of brief and frenzied courses and bouts. For the spectator of a play, the low standings would provide small improvement in his viewing of activity upon a raised stage, and the grate would be a constant irritation.

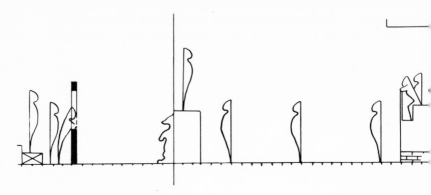

3. A schematic comparison of viewing conditions in a baiting amphitheatre and a playhouse. See note.

My reference above to the Swan drawing might remind us that there was available an alternative system to the grate for protecting the spectator, far more expensive to construct than a simple grated baiting ring when that was all that was needed, but possibly less costly when the Beargarden had become more elaborate in its accommodations for audiences. In the earliest royal and aristocratic bear-baitings, the few spectators were easily and safely accommodated at a window or gallery of a manor house overlooking a courtyard, or in the small raised houses for spectators at tiltyards; in both the principle was the same—the spectator was well above harm's way. In other words, if the lowest level of standings or seated gallery were high enough above the baiting space, and railed about, safety could be adequately provided without a grate; and there could be the added advantage that in adopting this feature from the playhouses an impediment would be removed to the viewing of plays as well. That is, of course, exactly the system elected by the builders of the Hope (where spectators would not have been in the yard during baitings) and probably for exactly that reason. The Hope was not a conversion of the old Beargarden, it was not rebuilt on the same foundations nor even on the same site, and it was not built from the same materials, which went to the carpenter Katherens, who was to pull downe all that [g]ame place or house . . . commonlie called . . . the Bearegarden [and] newly erect, build and sett vpp one other [g]ame place or Plaihouse fitt . . . both for players to play in and for the game of Beares and Bulls to be bayted in the same . . . ; And shall newe build . . . the said plaie house or game place neere or vppon the said place where the said game place did heretofore stand.[17]

(In the Hope contract the old single-purpose Beargarden is never referred to as a playhouse, only as a "game place"; the new dual-purpose building is never referred to as just a "game place" but consistently as "the playhouse or game place." Is it possible that the writers of this contract knew just what they were saying and said it precisely?)

The Hope contract says that, as at the Swan, the lowest gallery was to be set up on a brick foundation which was to rise 13 inches above the ground and that the posts for that gallery were to be 12 feet high; if the floor of the lower gallery was only 4 feet above the foundation then the rail would be 3 feet higher, a total of 8 feet above the ground level. Perhaps it was this particular feature of the Swan, a first gallery well above the yard, that made it a suitable model for the new multi-use amphitheatre, rather than a conjectured (and, on the evidence, unlikely) removable stage.

Did specialized theatres evolve from multi-use auditoria? Was the Theatre a multi-use "game house"? As far as I can tell, the latter speculation rests in part on a series of analogies and the former is a generalization from them. It is alleged that the Theatre was a multi-use amphitheatre in part because it was thought that the Swan was, but it was thought that the Swan was in part because the Hope was. Occasionally it is useful to come up for air, or down from the clouds, to observe that there is not a scintilla of real evidence that either the Theatre or the Swan (or the Curtain, the Rose, the Globe, the Fortune, etc.) was built to accommodate both exhibitions that required a stage and performances that required the absence of a stage. The only indisputable evidence we have for a multi-use auditorium, the Hope, seems to show clearly that it was uniquely designed to be so, that it remained one of its kind, and that it came at the end of an evolution in the Beargarden that was characterized by increasingly important borrowings from the public playhouses.[18] We do have evidence that the Hope was the venue for plays and fencing shows as well as for baitings—there are independent records of performances of these there on specific dates—but the Hope is the only amphitheatre of the period for which such evidence exists.

That points to the final kind of evidence I wish to present. What J. S. Mill called concomitant variation and we call positive correlation exists between plays and fencing shows to a very high degree; while fencers did not perform in all the play-houses, apparently (there is no record that private playhouses showed fencing matches, for instance), after about 1570 and until the Civil War, the fencers in London showed only where plays were also performed.[19] On the other hand, and with the concomitant variation of the Hope, there is no correlation between plays and fencing shows on the one hand (performances using a stage) and baitings on the other: there is no record of a play performed in a baiting ring, there is no record of a fencing show in a baiting ring, and there is no record of a baiting in a playhouse.

In *Early English Stages*, ii, part i, Glynne Wickham argues that the Theatre, indeed all the public playhouses, were multi-use auditoria; about conditions just before the erection of the Theatre, he says:

> Popular enthusiasm for stage-plays was keen enough to make substantial investment of capital in them a very enticing proposition, but the speculator who was willing to take the initial risk of putting his money into a building devoted to the acting of these plays had the strongest possible incentive to ensure that, should stage-plays be finally banned, his auditorium was so situated and so designed that it could continue to bring in a dividend from other forms of play, game [he means by this to include baiting] or recreation.

Since Professor Wickham believes that the baiting arena was a typical Elizabethan amphitheatre but without a stage and tiring-house,[20] this economic argument ought to have compelled Burbage to purchase or lease a beargarden instead of building the Theatre. Why didn't he?

Notes

1. *The Development of the English Playhouse* (Ithaca, 1973), pp. 26–27.
2. *The Globe Restored* (New York, 1954), p. 37.
3. Payne's ring was probably built between 1552 and 1557. He leased the property for ninety-nine years in 1540 (W. W. Braines, *The Site of the Globe Playhouse, Southwark* [London, 1924], p. 90) but probably would not have had access to the royal game until his partnership was formed with Simon Poulter, who is first recorded as Yeoman of the Queen's Bears in 1557 (J. P. Collier, *History of English Dramatic Poetry* [London, 1831], i, 161–62). John Allen was apparently still the Yeoman and was still baiting the royal game as late as 1552 (P.R.O., L.R.2/190). Payne operated his ring until he died in 1574 or 1575. Next in longevity must have been the bull- and bear-baiting ring of Robert Wistowe, who was cited for nonpayment of rent for "the bear yard" in a Chancery suit in 1559 (C.3/139/4) and who apparently baited there until 1575. Since no other baiting places are known to have had such permanence as Payne's and Wistowe's, these are the most likely models for the baiting rings depicted in the map views. Wistowe had no access to the royal game until he acquired Payne's ring from Payne's widow; therefore he must have depended upon bull-baiting primarily, with only an occasional itinerant bearward providing the means for bear-baiting.
4. C.3/139/4; E.134/18 Jas.I/Mich./10, Crown Interrogatory #15; Dulwich MS. viii, ff. 43, 44; C. L. Kingsford, "Paris Garden and the Bearbaiting," *Archaeologia*, second series, xx (1920): 171–72.
5. O. L. Brownstein, "The Popularity of Baiting in England before 1600," *Educational Theatre Journal* xxi, no. 3 (1969): 247–49. In *Early English Stages* (London, 1972), ii, ii, 56n, Professor Wickham remarks that he cannot find the evidence for this conclusion; my article summarizes the argument, but the interested reader would have to consult the documents cited in the footnotes for the evidence, which includes every datable record of baiting in London between 1500 and 1600. My assumption is that no mad scholar systematically destroyed every document that would permit the dating of a commercial baiting on a non-

holiday week-day; the consistency of independent datable records of commercial baiting days creates a high degree of probability for the conclusion that commercial baitings were
conducted on Sundays and holidays exclusively in this period.
An extended treatment of the subject can be found in my dis-
sertation, "Stake and Stage" (University of Iowa, 1963), pp.
76–90.

6. "The Popularity of Baiting in England before 1600," p. 247.
7. Ibid., p. 248; E. K. Chambers, *The Elizabethan Stage* (Oxford, 1923), II, 451.
8. Kingsford, p. 172.
9. Though ultimately a trivial matter I once went to a great deal of trouble to get it straight; see "Stake and Stage," pp. 43–55. The royal game park in Paris Garden Manor was the permanent home for the Queen's bears and mastiffs, and its Keepership was synonomous with the Mastership of the Game of Bears, Dogs, and Apes—thus the official title was Master of the Game at (or in or of) Paris Garden. In 1608 Alleyn and Henslowe leased three-and-a-half acres in Lambeth, very probably in order to relocate the game park; the lease is endorsed by Alleyn "beargarden," and 1608 is the last year in which the Treasurer of the Chamber uses the title "Master of his Majesty's Game at Paris Garden."
10. "The Popularity of Baiting," pp. 241–44.
11. *Letters and Papers, Foreign and Domestic, . . . Henry VIII*, XXI, ii, 88, 328.
12. "Stake and Stage," chap. IV, pp. 109–78, treats the methods and the available pictorial documents relevant to the interpretation of these drawings and those of William Smith.
13. G. F. Warner, *Catalogue of the Manuscripts and Muniments . . . at Dulwich* (London, 1881), p. 82.
14. Giles Dawson, "London's Bull-Baiting and Bear-Baiting Arena in 1562," *Shakespeare Quarterly* xv (1964), no. 1: 97–101.
15. Req.2/108/5; E.134/18 Jas.I/Mich./10, John Taylor, answer #14; Kingsford, pp. 171–72.
16. My reasons for this inference: in the document last referred to in note 15, Crown Interrogatory #14 suggests that Payne's ring was unique in having standings:

> Did you knowe or haue yo^u heard of certaine scaffolds or standinges heretofore erected or set vp for people to stand to see the bayting of the beares, were they comonly called m^r Paynes Standings . . . [?]

Wistowe, who had a baiting arena to the west of Payne's, immediately on the latter's death abandoned his own and purchased Payne's. Finally, the most credible explanation I have for
the absence of any suggestion of standings around the baiting

rings in the map views is that only one of the rings had them
(the standings are amply documented), and therefore, consistent
with the contemporary concept of maps as schemata, where
there were two of something, peculiarities in one were either
added to the other or eliminated, so that the two were made
to look alike. Thus in the Braun and Hogenberg, the Smith,
and the Agas, though the depictions differ among the views, the
two baiting rings are presented as identical within each view,
with identical kennels, ponds, bear houses, and even size of the
properties. Even if one of the views were "correct" in its doubled
depiction, then the other two, each doubly "wrong," would still
demonstrate the principle; but such symmetry in the model is
so improbable as to defy calculation. Payne's standings must
have been perceived as temporary and not *essential* by contemporary map-makers. The narrowness of the property on
which Payne's ring was built, 31 feet, suggests that, unless the
ring was very small, the likelihood is that when the standings
were added they were not built around the complete circuit of
the grate; however, the property was 70 feet deep north and
south, and the standings may have been placed at one or both
of those compass points. A standing to the north of the ring
would have been mere background clutter to a topographical
artist. We should also be alert to the possibility that Wistowe's
"bull baiting," the western ring in the map views, was not in
fact as high as Payne's—that is, this symmetry, too, might be
a product of schematic rendering. Wistowe did not bait the royal
game until he took Payne's ring, and therefore he must have
depended largely on bull-baiting at his own establishment.

17. Edward Alleyn testified that the greater size of the Hope would
    require that it overlap the plot leased from the Bishop of Win-
    chester (on which the Beargarden stood) and the larger plot to
    the south leased from another landlord, so it was decided to
    build the Hope entirely on the land south of the Bishop of
    Winchster's property (*Early English Stages*, ii, i, 362).

18. The Theatre and Curtain were apparently built with two upper
    stories of galleries in 1576; in 1583 the Beargarden had a single
    upper story, probably an upper standing, and was rebuilt in that
    year "in stead of the said scaffolds or standings [with] certaine
    galleries . . . about the said bayting place . . . larger in Circuit &
    compasse then the fformer called m^r Paynes Standing" (E.134/
    18 Jas.i/Mich./10, Crown Interrogatory #15). The next develop-
    ment of the Beargarden was its transformation into the Hope,
    when it adopted the tiring-house, heavens, stage, and, as I have
    argued above, the raised first-level seated gallery from the play-
    house.

19. O. L. Brownstein, "A Record of London Inn-Playhouses from

c.1565–1590," *Shakespeare Quarterly* xxII (1971), no. 1: 20, 22–23.
20. Pp. 171, 161, 163.

Notes to Illustrations

Fig. 2. Smith wrote *A breffe description of the Royall Citie of London . . . 1575*, a manuscript account of London, now in the British Museum, which is identical to that in *A Particular Description*. It does not contain a drawing of the city, but there is also in the B.M. (Crace #374) a hand-drawn profile view of London, identical to that in *A Particular Description*, which is signed "W.S. f[ecit]." This drawing is attributed to William Stuckley, but it is surely Smith's for *A breffe description*. This is one of his free-hand drawings from nature, like his published drawings of Rochester, Stafford, Lichfield, and Coventry.

Fig. 3. The baiting amphitheatre is represented by its lowest level only. Without the standings the condition is identical to that shown in the Braun and Hogenberg and the Smith views, and with them we should have an approximation of William Payne's "low standings." In order to make an extreme test of sight lines, I have made the ring in this drawing only 20 feet in diameter, smaller than an actual baiting ring is likely to have been. The standing is shown only one foot high for the same reason. On the playhouse side, the first gallery is 12 feet high above a 13-inch brick foundation; the lowest floor of this gallery is 3 feet above the foundation, the lowest seat 18 inches above the floor, the front rail 3 feet high, and the gallery 20 feet from the front edge of the stage (sight lines to an activity on a raised stage are not affected by distance).

A Handlist of Documents about the Theatre in Shoreditch

Herbert Berry

For more than 130 years we have been alluding to and arguing over the documentation for the first regular playhouse, the Theatre, built in Shoreditch more than 400 years ago. More documentation has been found for the Theatre than, with the possible exception of the Boar's Head, any other public playhouse, and since 1913 most of this documentation has been available in printed form, unlike the documentation for any other playhouse, even now. Yet no one seems to have looked at the originals for some sixty years. No one seems to have wondered if the printed transcriptions are accurate, no one seems to have asked if one could find yet more, and no one seems even to have asked whether many of the citations used so long ago would, if written on tickets today, cause the proper documents to be produced. I propose here to survey the documents, assess the printed transcriptions, announce a new document or two, and give the current citations for them all. For since 1913 many of the numbers have been changed, and in some cases the new ones (now themselves sixty or more years old) are by no means easy to establish.

J. P. Collier published the first notices of documents about the Theatre, in his *Memoirs of the Principal Actors in the Plays of Shakespeare* of 1846, and more three years later in his article, "Original History of 'The Theatre,' in Shoreditch, and Connexion of the Burbadge Family with it."[1] Perhaps luckily, Collier had not found them himself. A Mr. Monro, one of the registrars of Chancery, had found those which Collier used in the book, and F. Devon of the Chapter House, Westminster, those in the article. Before the Public Record Office opened in 1866, such public records were kept in, among other places, the Roll's Chapel in Chancery Lane, the Chapter House, and the Tower. Collier misunderstood the documents and did not pursue them. Indeed, he thought those in the book referred to Blackfriars. He corrected himself in the article, but in reprintings of the book as late as 1879,[2] the documents there still concerned Blackfriars. It was his younger contemporary, J. O. Halliwell-Phillipps, who fully realized what Collier had been given and who set out to find more of the same. He found some of the better things, which he used discriminatingly, beginning in the second edition of his *Outlines of the Life of Shakespeare* (1882). Document work was still in its infancy, however, so that Halliwell-Phillipps missed some citations completely, gave others inadequately, and used the documents less fully than he could have done. Moreover, he by no means exhausted the hoard, and without some of the documents which he could have found but did not, his understanding of those which he did find was necessarily imperfect.

The documents about the Theatre then became much of the fuel of the competition in the Round Room of the Public Record Office between the American, C. W. Wallace, and the redoubtable Scottish lady, Mrs. C. C. Stopes (mother of the even more redoubtable Marie Stopes), in the years before the First World War. Wallace and his energetic wife, Hulda, worked across the room from Mrs. Stopes, both parties striving to obscure their work from the other and at the same time to find what the other was doing. Needless to say, both parties ransacked the classes of documents from which Collier's and Halliwell-Phillipps's documents had come. Between them, they found everything there which their predecessors had used and much more. They also pressed into other classes of documents and found yet more. Both parties published books in 1913 about their work, in which they revealed what they had been doing in the Round Room and, inevitably, altered dramatically the case at the Theatre.[3] All too often they revealed that they had been at work on the same documents, but, fortunately, they also revealed that the Wallaces had spent a good deal of their time among matters of which Mrs. Stopes had not known, and that Mrs. Stopes had spent some of hers among a few unknown to the Wallaces. The Wallaces quite clearly had the better of everything to which both they and Mrs. Stopes had put their hands, but because Mrs. Stopes had dealt with some documents unknown to the Wallaces, her book is still useful, though these documents are much less important than the others.

W. W. Braines then set out to locate in the London of his day exactly where the Theatre had stood. He was "a principal officer" in the Department of the Clerk of the London County Council, and his work was the result of a suggestion made in the council in 1914. (As the result of another suggestion made in the council in 1921, he was also to locate the site of the Globe.) Braines reviewed the Wallaces' work carefully but could not extend it. He reviewed those parts of Mrs. Stopes's work of which the Wallaces had not known and managed to find considerably more than she had done. The London County Council issued his work as a pamphlet in the series, *Indication of Houses of Historical Interest in London*, in 1915, but Braines continued to think about the matter and to go back to the documents. He issued his work himself with significant revisions in 1917,[4] and the London County Council issued it again, with more significant revisions, in the section of the *Survey of London* dealing with Shoreditch, for which Braines was responsible (vol. viii, 1922). The London County Council reissued the work as a pamphlet in 1923, in the same series as the original one (part xliii) but with the revisions of 1922 and a few more; and this version appeared without further change in 1930. Braines thought of this version of 1923 (p. 9) as a somewhat abbreviated form of that of 1922, so that the final version must be a conflation of the two. Though neither a literary man nor a historian by profession, he became one of the most astute and successful of workers among documents, and only partly because he severely limited his objectives. He seems to have been the last person who fingered, at least for publication, the documents about the Theatre.

Collier, Halliwell-Phillipps, and Braines used documents as most writers do, to substantiate assertions. So they merely quoted these documents here and there, alluded to them, paraphrased them. Thanks to their warfare in the Round Room, however, Wallace and Mrs. Stopes apparently strove to get their findings into print before the other did. They probably felt that they could not afford the time which an elaborate study of their documents would require. Both their books are, therefore, mainly a succession of transcriptions, especially Wallace's. Between them, they printed transcriptions of all the really important documents. All Braines's documents extend the lines of inquiry in which Mrs. Stopes had worked and Wallace had not. Braines's documents, therefore, are not the crucial ones. They have to do with a then ancient argument about the land on which the Theatre stood and a then new one about a neighbouring site, both very useful for his purpose but not for ours, if ours concerns the playhouse itself. Chambers reviewed all these matters in his *Elizabethan Stage* of 1923. He pointed out that the documents concern four separate legal quarrels, each quarrel consisting of numerous lawsuits and other legal ploys, and none of the quarrels materially overlapping any of the others. He put each document, therefore, into one of four categories, which he called A, B, C, and D.

Category A is a long series of lawsuits beginning in the early 1580s and not ending from our point of view until 1612. It concerns who owned the land on which the Theatre stood. Mrs. Stopes and Braines found all these documents, except for a few which I have found.[5] The litigation was extensive, and almost certainly more documents remain to be found. Category B is a series of lawsuits from 1596 to 1604 about the ownership of an adjoining piece of property once leased by the Burbages. It has little to do with the playhouse. Mrs. Stopes and Braines found all these documents, too, except for those which I have found. Probably more of these also remain to be found. Category C is a series of lawsuits from 1586 to 1597 between the Burbages and their partner in building the playhouse, John Brayne, and his successors. Mrs. Stopes and Wallace competed fiercely for these documents in Category C, and Wallace conspicuously had the better of the competition. Category D is a series of lawsuits from 1599 to 1602 between the Burbages and their landlord in Shoreditch, Giles Allen, over the Burbages' pulling down of the Theatre in the Christmas season of 1598–99 and their carting it away to Southwark for re-erecting as the Globe. Mrs. Stopes and Wallace competed here, too, and once again Wallace had vastly the better of the competition. Perhaps the best general discussion of all these lawsuits has been that by J. Q. Adams in his *Shakespearean Playhouses* (1917).

Wallace is among the great figures of the P.R.O., and his work about the Theatre is among his most thorough, sensible, and practised. He went through vast piles of paper and parchment, pursuing not only the main documents of a case, but also the supporting and arcane ones. If we are to find significant new documents in the matters which Wallace studied, we must do so by strokes of luck and not by systematically carrying the work farther than he did. Mrs. Stopes was not nearly so thorough or patient.

Moreover, the Wallaces' transcribing is systematically rigorous, and it is generally accurate, especially in the really major documents, such as the bills and answers and the depositions. On page after page of theirs, one can find relatively little to which he might seriously object. They are less accurate, however, in the supporting documents, such as the decrees and orders of the various courts. I have looked letter for letter at more than 2,000 lines of the Wallaces (as they printed them), including at least part of every numbered item below. I reckon that they made a mistake in only one line out of nine or ten among the most important documents in English, the bills and answers and depositions, but one line out of just over five among the decrees and orders, at all of which I looked. They made one mistake in about four lines of Latin, but there the work is much more difficult, and the Wallaces' reconstruction of so much abbreviated Latin must remain a tour de force of its kind. It is one thing to go over transcriptions of such difficult material; it is quite another to read it with nothing before one but the text. Wallace must have done the Latin himself. Could he also have done the important things in English himself and passed the others to his wife? Or vice versa?

In any event, even where they are not perfect, they missed spellings and sometimes punctuation, but rarely the sense. For example, in one order of the Court of Chancery, the Wallaces made seven mistakes in the thirteen lines of the document as they printed it (C.33/81/f.493^v, Wallaces' pp. 64–65):

Lines	The Wallaces	The Document
3–4	"hathe in"	"haue put in"
4–5	"Insuffycynt"	"Insuffycyent"
5	"showinge"	"shewinge"
5	"cause"	"causes"
9	"demurrer"	"demorrer"
9	"suffycynt"	"suffycyent"

and in the marginal entry they left out "Myles" after "Robte" (they seem to have added it by mistake to the marginal entry at f. 720^v, their p. 65). This is their worst patch of transcription which I have noticed. In an order of the Court of Requests, they did nearly as badly, eleven mistakes in twenty-three lines as they printed the document (Req.1/49/22 Apr. 42 Eliz., their pp. 205–6):

Lines	The Wallaces	The Document
1	"Cuthbert"	"Cuthberte"
5	"Iniunccion"	"Iniunction"
6	"one"	"m^r"
6	"seuerallye"	"seuerally"
7–8	"Accordingly"	"Accordingely"
9	"is"	"ys"
9	"counsail"	"counsaill"
10	"furthwth"	"furthewth"
19	"therof"	"thereof"
21	"is"	"ys"
23	"heard"	"hearde"

Rather hasty transcribing as the bells were ringing at the end of the day? In transcribing their other nineteen orders of Chancery and Requests, they made some forty-five mistakes in 289 lines, or one in about six and a half lines, but only one mistake is important (see C-26 below).[6]

Mrs. Stopes could do much worse. For a start, she was not systematic. She often modernized spelling, capitalization, and punctuation, but by no means always, and when she has an old spelling it not infrequently is an invention of her own. She too often abstracted documents when she seems to be transcribing them, reading, for example, "at lardge" where the document reads "more at lardge," and "on behalf" for "on the behalf," and "that the said" for "that then the said" (E.123/27/f.110ᵛ, her p. 189). Moreover, she usually wrote the abbreviation for page when she meant that for folio, and sometimes got dates wrong by a year or so, or left them so vague that the reader can get them right only by luck. In another document, for example, she has "enformed" where the document has "informed," "defts." where the document has no abbreviation, "unpublisht" where the document has "vnpublished," "each parties" for "each partie," "shalle" for "shalbe"—all perhaps rather unimportant. But in the same document she read "he could not have his commission readie" where the document reads "he could not haue his Commissioners readie," and "not concerned in the bill" where the document reads "not conteyned in the bill" (E.123/28/f.270ᵛ, her p. 194).

In one list of names, she read "Philip," "Gobourne," and "Brymefield" where the document reads "Phillipp," "Goborne," and "Bromefeyld," and she omitted a name after Bromefeyld, "William Furnis." In another list of the same kind, she read "Oliver Lilt" for "Oliver Talte" and "Maye" for "May"; and in yet another list in the same series, she read "Robert Myles, gent." and "Raff Myles, gent." for "Roberte Myles gent" and "Raffe Myles gent" (Req.1/188/Easter 42 Eliz./9 Apr. 42 Eliz. [1600];/Trin. 42 Eliz./23 May 42 Eliz.; her pp. 216–17). In one document which she shared with the Wallaces, she got the folio right (454) when the Wallaces bungled it (485), a triumph, perhaps. But she got the date wrong, 22

February for 17 February (C.33/77/f.454, Wallace's p. 46, Stopes's pp. 159–60).

Although Stopes's imperfections are more persistent and more serious than the Wallaces', they do not render her book useless. For her transcriptions almost always get the matter generally right if not right in detail. Her practices with spelling, capitalization, and punctuation, not to say omission, are so capricious, however, that it is probably safer to paraphrase rather than to quote her transcriptions. In longer and more arduous documents, she regularly left out the *pro forma* things and added words of her own for clarity, and in these places she clearly meant her work not as transcription, but sensible abstracting (for example, Ward 13/B.29/16–19 from the end, her pp. 166–70). This particular document is so trying, that one should probably be more grateful than censorious. Her work in general is simply on a lower order of rigour and accuracy than the Wallaces', and it is not surprising that Braines could carry her work farther than she did.

In the Handlist, I have grouped the documents about the Theatre into Chambers's four categories, summarizing the quarrel which a category records, then listing the documents in that category, call number by call number, in chronological order, as though each call number represents one document. Following each call number the places are cited where Collier, Halliwell-Phillipps, Wallace, Stopes, and Braines transcribed or quoted the matters included in the call number. Then there is a summary of those matters. Where a call number includes more than one document, I use the document with the earliest date for the chronological scheme and list the documents included. One call number can include as many as eighteen or more documents dated over many months (see D-7). All call numbers are the current ones, rather than those which Wallace and the others used. I cite the first editions of Collier's book and article, the seventh of Halliwell-Phillipps's book (1887), and the version of 1923 of Braines's work. Except for a photographic reprint by Blom in 1969, Wallace's book has not been reissued, nor, except for a reprint by Haskell House in 1970, has Mrs. Stopes's book.

Where a significant document is missing but its contents are clear from remarks in other documents, I cite the document as though it exists, giving the word "Missing" in lieu of a call number and adding in parentheses the documents which describe this one. For documents not previously reported, the phrase "Not yet used" appears in lieu of the works by Wallace and the rest. I modernize people's Christian names but spell their surnames as they usually appear in the documentation, preferring the spelling of a signature if there is one.[7] Exceptions are the Burbages, Richard and Cuthbert, who signed themselves "Burbadge"; and Giles Allen, who signed himself "Gyles Aleyn" and whom Wallace called "Gyles Allen" and Mrs. Stopes "Giles Alleyn." Where I have noticed a mistake in the Wallaces' transcribing which materially affects meaning, I mention it in the remarks about the document. But I have not looked letter by letter at the whole of every document, hence have by no means caught every mistake.

My remarks about some aspects especially of Categories A and B, but also C and D, reflect, often silently, a reading of the documents different from that of previous writers.

Category A

This legal quarrel concerned the ownership of the land on which the Theatre stood. A family named Webb had acquired it from the Crown in 1544 and then made it part of a marriage contract with a family named Peckham in 1554. The marriage took place and the property passed to the Peckhams. In 1555 they sold it to a family named Bumpsted, who in the same year mortgaged it for £300 to a family named Allen. In the next year the Bumpsteds took another £300 from the Allens and let them have it. Now Giles Allen owned the property, or thought he did, and it was Giles Allen who was the Burbages's landlord. In 1582 the Peckhams began a long legal fight to regain the property, arguing mainly that though the marriage had taken place in 1554, it had not taken place before Michaelmas in that year as it was supposed to do in the marriage contract. Therefore the Peckhams could not sell it to the Bumpsteds, who could not sell it to the Allens. Allen fought valiantly, but, as Braines found, the Peckhams actually won the fight. For while Allen still had it when he died, on March 27, 1608 (A-15), the Peckhams sold the place with an apparently good title in March 1612. Braines thought this turn of events incredible, but one of his own documents explains how it happened. Braines must not have read the document very carefully. It is a sheet on which in about 1582 the Peckhams summarized their case for their own purposes. In the last lines they explained how they really expected to get the land back. They offered to buy it for as much as the Allens had paid the Bumpsteds. Or as the document concludes: "Note that this pl*aintiff* [the Peckhams] offereth the defendant [Giles Allen] for the discharge of his fathers Couen*a*nte wth Bumsted asmuche mony as he receaued for the land so that consideringe the meane proffits wch he hath receaued now xxvi yeres, the defendant can be no loser by it" (see A-11). The lawsuits were only ways of putting pressure on Allen and keeping the price down. Eventually Allen's widow must have made some deal with the Peckhams and quietly passed the property to them.

A-1. British Museum, Cotton MS. Vesp. F III, no. 38 (Braines, p. 8): A letter of July 23, 1544, from Queen Katherine Parr to an unnamed recipient. The King had meant to grant all of Holywell Priory to Henry Webb, gentleman usher of her privy chamber, but Webb got only part. She desired the recipient's favour in Webb's behalf. (Braines used this letter as it appears in Dugdale's *Monasticon*, 1846, IV, 392; the original is abstracted in *Letters and Papers, Foreign and Domestic, . . . Henry VIII*, XIX, i, #967.)

A-2. C.66/747/m.41–42 (not yet used): A patent by which the Webbs acquired for £81 part of the land in Holywell Priory on which the Theatre eventually stood: August 5, 1544. (Noted in *Letters and Papers, Foreign and Domestic, . . . Henry VIII*, XIX, ii, #166(7).)

A-3. C.66/740/m.4–5 (not yet used): A patent by which the Webbs acquired for £55 the rest of the land (see A-2) in Holywell Priory on which the Theatre eventually stood: September 23, 1544. (Noted in *Letters and Papers, Foreign and Domestic, . . . Henry VIII*, XIX, ii, #340(33); see also #586.)

A-4. E.371/324/#70 (Braines, p. 9): A copy of the patent of September 23, 1544 (A-3), kept in the Exchequer.

A-5. C.54/516/m.8–9 (Braines, p. 9): The entry on the close roll of the contract, dated August 16, 1555, by which the Peckhams sold to Christopher Bumpsted for £533.6s.8d. the land in Holywell Priory on which the Theatre eventually stood.

A-6. C.P.25(2)/74/629/2–3 P&M/Mich./no.50 (not yet used): A fine of 1555 by which the Peckhams acknowledged that they had sold to Christopher Bumpsted the land on which the Theatre eventually stood.

A-7. C.54/521/m.12–13 (Braines, p. 9): The entry on the close roll of the contract, dated November 1, 1555, by which Christopher Bumpsted mortgaged to Christopher Allen and his son, Giles, the land in Holywell Priory on which the Theatre eventually stood. The Allens had paid £300 and would pay £300 more on April 4, 1556, if they wanted to buy the property, if Bumpsted wanted to sell it, and if Bumpsted could give them a good title.

A-8. C.54/521/m.13 (not yet used): A bond of £700 of November 1, 1555, by which Christopher Bumpsted guaranteed performance of his part of the contract of the same date (A-7).

A-9. C.3/9/82 (Braines, p. 9): A lawsuit in Chancery in which Christopher Bumpsted sued Giles Allen so as to stop a lawsuit of Allen's at common law against Bumpsted. The Allens had, apparently, advanced Bumpsted the second £300 on the land in Holywell Priory on which the Theatre eventually stood (A-7,8; B-5), but found that it was not worth what Bumpsted had claimed, that Bumpsted was unwilling to draw a second contract conveying the property to the Allens, and that Bumpsted would not give the Allens the documents which would guarantee their title. Bumpsted denied all these claims. Documents: the bill (October 9, 1562), and Allen's answer and Bumpsted's replication (both undated).

A-10. E.13/344/25 (Braines, p. 23): A summary of the Peckhams' first lawsuit against Giles Allen, in the Court of Exchequer of Pleas, Easter 1582.

A-11. British Museum, Lansdowne MS. III, f.101 (or, in another series of foliation, f.110) (Braines, p. 23): A summary of their case (A-10) drawn up by the Peckhams for their own use, c. 1582.

A-12. Ward 13/B.29 [16–19 from the end] (Stopes, pp. 166–70): The Peckhams' second lawsuit against Giles Allen, in the Court of Wards because the elder Peckham (Edmund) had died and his son (George) was a royal ward. Documents: the bill (June 9, 1589), Allen's reply (October 20, 1589), Edmund Peckham's replication (October 31, 1589), and Allen's rejoinder (November 28, 1589).

A-13. Ward 9/86/f.159–60 (Braines, p. 23): A summary of the Peckhams' lawsuit against Giles Allen in the Court of Wards (A-12), and the Court's decision to dismiss it: Michaelmas 1591 (after November 16).

A-14. K.B.27/1377/m.253 (Braines, p. 23): A summary dated Hilary 1603 of a lawsuit in the King's Bench which may constitute the Peckhams' third against Giles Allen. The Peckhams had leased several houses in Shoreditch to John Hollingworth on November 10, 1602, and now Hollingworth sued three men (John Goodgame, William Rowe, and James Kelley) for trespass on the premises. Braines identified the men as Allen's tenants, though the document does not, and presumed, therefore, that the houses were part of Allen's domain in Holywell. In a companion lawsuit (summarized on the next membrane), Hollingworth also sued Cuthbert Burbage at the same time and on the same occasion, yet Burbage does not seem to have been a tenant of Allen's after the winter of 1598–99.

A-15. C.142/309/#163 (Stopes, *Notes & Queries*, Oct. 30, 1909, p. 343; Braines, *Survey of London*, VIII, 171): The inquisition post mortem taken July 16, 1608, on Giles Allen, showing that when he died he still owned the property in Holywell on which the Theatre had stood. (Braines, oddly, got the date of Allen's death wrong by a year. According to this document, he died on March 27, 1608; his widow took administration of his goods on April 21, 1608: PROB.6/7/f.111ᵛ.)

A-16. C.54/2128/m.20 (Braines, p. 23): The entry on the close roll of the contract of March 10, 1612, by which the Peckhams sold the property in Holywell on which the Theatre had stood.

Note. Braines, in *Survey of London*, VIII, 171, offered a fine of 1610 to show that the Peckhams by then owned the property in Holywell on which the Theatre had stood; but while the fine mentions George Peckham, it does not mention property specifically in Holywell and so cannot be taken as necessarily referring to that on which the Theatre had stood: C.P. 25(2)/323/7 Jas. I/Hil./4.

Category B

This quarrel was about whether Giles Allen or the Earls of Rutland owned a part of Holywell Priory consisting of two buildings and an open space at the sides of which they lay. The buildings were a barn (anciently, but no longer, called the oat barn) and a stable. The open space was the "void ground or yard," as it is called in one lawsuit (B-5, 10), or the inner court of the Priory, as it is called in another (B-8, 9). A great barn undeniably Allen's was on the north side of this void ground, the stable was on the east side, the oat barn was on the south side, and the Priory wall was on the west side. The oat barn, stable, and void ground should have belonged to Allen, because they had belonged to his predecessors, being specifically mentioned in Henry Webb's patent of 1544 (A-3) and not mentioned in any of the Earls' leases (see B-1).

In 1539, however, before the Priory had been dissolved, the prioress and convent had leased the oat barn and stable to Richard Manners for twenty years. He became Sir Richard, and he must have been a relative of the Earls of Rutland. Along with the oat barn and stable, Manners had got "convenient rome betwene" and ingress, egress, and regress—the use, that is, of the void ground. This lease is mentioned in Webb's patent as an encumbrance on his property. Though it expired in 1559, four years after the Allens had acquired their part of Holywell, the Earls of Rutland evidently continued to occupy the buildings and use the ground, and they came to assume that the buildings and, eventually, even the ground belonged to their part of Holywell.

Allen suffered this state of affairs for many years, resigning himself, it seems, to the loss of his buildings but not to the loss of his void ground. At least once he rented part of the void ground to a tenant of his in the great barn, and he included the whole of the void ground with the premises which he leased to the Burbages for, among other things, the building of the Theatre. In his lease to the Burbages (see B-2 and Wallace, pp. 170–71), however, he mentioned the oat barn and stable as occupied by the Rutlands and he did not include them among the leased premises; in a lawsuit of 1601 (B-8) he mentioned those buildings as "by some of the Earles of Rutland . . . wth houlden from" him.

During all these years the void ground lay for the most part open and used by anyone having business in that part of Holywell. The Burbages built their playhouse not on the void ground, but immediately north of the great barn, the north side of which they shored against the playhouse. Then, the Rutlands having ceased to live in Holywell, the current Earl leased his part of it to his steward, Thomas Screven, who set about capitalizing the void ground. He rented the two buildings and the ground for a short term to John Powell and Richard Robinson (two saltpetremen who were making the stuff in the oat barn), who with a labourer, Roger Amyes, seized (that is, no doubt, fenced off) part of the void ground on May 1, 1596, and kept it until June 27.

Allen decided at last to act, and the Burbages decided to help him. Urged on by Allen, the Burbages sued Powell, Robinson, and Amyes at once in the King's Bench for trespass in the barn and on the ground. Screven hastened in the Earl's name to sue the Burbages in the Court of Wards (the current Earl being a minor) in an effort, which was successful, to get the lawsuit in the King's Bench stopped. On July 20 Screven leased the ground and both buildings to John Knapp for twenty years for a fee of £50 and £14.14s.8d. a year, and Powell and Robinson continued making saltpetre in the barn. When the Earl came of age on October 6, 1597, the lawsuit in Wards perforce ceased. The Burbages and Allen then pressed the lawsuit in King's Bench. Screven did his best to delay it, but first he gave the Burbages and Allen something more to sue him about. On November 2 Powell and Robinson, now joined by Knapp, once again seized part of the void ground, this time building a mud-wall around that part and keeping it. The Burbages and Allen

managed to bring the lawsuit in King's Bench to the point of a
decisive hearing early in the winter of 1598–99, but just as
they did so, Screven (using the Earl's name) sued them again,
this time in the Court of Exchequer King's Remembrancer, and
again got the lawsuit in King's Bench stopped. He took his
business to that court, he said, because the disputed premises
were part of the Queen's inheritance and so a concern of the
Exchequer. Unlike Webb, that is, the Rutlands had not negoti-
ated a grant of their part of Holywell from the Crown but had
been content with a series of leases, first from the Priory and
then from the Crown. So the place had belonged to Henry VIII
on the dissolution of the Priory and had descended to Elizabeth. Coincidentally, or perhaps mainly, the point enabled
Screven to argue that the Burbages and Allen were trying to
deny the Queen a part of her inheritance.

Allen delayed answering this newest lawsuit for almost two
years, perhaps because from the Christmas season of 1598–99
he had his hands full with the Burbages, who had dismantled
the Theatre, carried it across the river, and rebuilt it as the
Globe. Allen had to be arrested, on October 22, 1600, to bring
him to answer the lawsuit in the Exchequer. He and Screven
then went expeditiously through the preliminary steps, but no
further. At the end of January 1601 Allen futilely asked the
court to dismiss Screven's lawsuit. To more purpose, Screven
and Knapp were presiding over a process of subleasing which
made Allen's task more difficult. Knapp leased the two buildings and the void ground to John Lewis on February 17, 1598.
The two of them then leased the oat barn and part of the void
ground to Richard Hill for £3 a year, and on April 23, 1601, Hill
leased his barn and ground to Francis Langley for thirteen or
fourteen years (Langley couldn't remember which) and £3 "&
odd monie" a year. (Langley also couldn't remember the first
name of Cuthbert Burbage.) Langley was the builder of the
Swan, and he was fresh from a similar, but much grander,
venture in disputed property at the Boar's Head. On May 16,
having brought along his man, John Johnson, and hired Amyes
and Lewis, Langley set about building a mudwall around his
part of the void ground, which, with the other walled part,
completely blocked that ground. Amyes left on other business,

and Allen and some tenants arrived to chase the rest away, but soon Langley returned and effectually fenced off his part of the ground.

Protesting that he already had legal fees "farre exceedinge the value of the said grounde," Allen now took the lot of them to the Star Chamber, as Richard Samwell had done at the Boar's Head the year before. But after most of the preliminaries were finished in November 1601, Allen seems to have lost interest in this lawsuit, too, and the Court seems to have given him no comfort.[8] In the summer and fall of 1602 Screven was pushing on with the case in the Exchequer, and Allen was ignoring it. In October he took momentary interest, but after that neither he nor Screven did anything for a year and a half. On April 30, 1604, finally, Allen asked the Court of Exchequer to dismiss the matter so that he could get on with his eight-year-old lawsuit in the King's Bench. The court decided a few days later that the matter should be heard during the first sitting of the next term. Whether it was heard or not (the documents are missing for that term), Allen gained nothing by it. He did not renew his lawsuit in the King's Bench, nor did he, it seems, repossess his two buildings and void ground, though his successor in Holywell was interested in them as late as 1615 (B-14).

The Burbages helped Allen against Screven even though at the same time they were arguing strenuously with Allen about the terms on which they might renew their lease. It expired in April 1597, and thereafter the Burbages rented the place without a lease. They must have thought that by helping Allen against Screven they might get a renewal on relatively favourable terms—provided, presumably, that the whole place did not prove to belong to the Peckhams.

B-1. E.303/11/Middx./no.5 (Braines, pp. 8, 14): A lease of April 1, 1539, in which Holywell Priory leased to Richard Manners (evidently a relative of the Earls of Rutland) for twenty years an oat barn and a stable with the use of the yard at the sides of which they lay. The Burbages and Giles Allen eventually quarrelled with Thomas Screven and the Earl of Rutland about the ownership of these premises. Allen thought that he owned them because his property in Holywell had specifically included them when his predecessor, Webb, had acquired it from the Crown in 1544, and this lease was then cited as an encumbrance on it (see Webb's patent, A-3). Moreover, they are not mentioned in the leases by which the Earls of Rutland held their part of Holywell: two from the Priory, November 8, 1537, and January 1, 1538 (L.R.1/47/f.205, 202), and a renewal from the Crown, December 18, 1584 (C.66/1267/m.29–30).

B-2. Missing (see B-3, 4, 5, 6; D-1): The lease of April 13, 1576, by which the Burbages leased parts of Holywell from Giles Allen as, among other things, a site for the Theatre. Included was the ground at the sides of which lay, not included, an oat barn and a stable; the ownership of these premises was eventually claimed by both Allen and the Earl of Rutland and their tenants. A draft renewal of the lease (November 1, 1585) is quoted, apparently completely, in D-1 (transcribed by Wallace, pp. 169–78), where at least the description of the property should be the same as in the original lease.

B-3. K.B.27/1353/m.320 (Halliwell-Phillipps, I, 351; Stopes, pp. 184–85): A summary of a lawsuit in the King's Bench in which Cuthbert Burbage sued three of Thomas Screven's tenants (John Powell, Richard Robinson, Roger Amyes) for trespass between May 1 and June 27, 1596, in the oat barn and on the ground beside which it lay. The ground was included among the parts of Holywell which the Burbages rented from Giles Allen. It and two adjoining buildings, the oat barn and a stable, were claimed by both Allen and the Earl of Rutland, who had leased them all to his steward, Screven. Burbage began the lawsuit in Trinity Term 1596, and the summary is dated January 15, 1599, by which time Powell et al. had pleaded not guilty and demanded trial, but the lawsuit had been postponed and no date set for trial.

B-4. Missing (see B-5, 8): A lawsuit in the Court of Wards in which Thomas Screven (in the name of the Earl of Rutland) sued Cuthbert Burbage and Giles Allen in a successful attempt to stop Burbage's lawsuit in the King's Bench (B-3). The lawsuit was filed in the summer of 1596 and, according to Allen, was the same as B-5. It was filed in Wards because the Earl was still a minor.

B-5. E.112/28/369 (Halliwell-Phillipps, I, 350; Stopes, pp. 185–89; Braines, pp. 9, 26n): A lawsuit in the Court of Exchequer King's Remembrancer in which Thomas Screven (in the name of the Earl of Rutland) sued Cuthbert Burbage and Giles (misnamed Richard) Allen in a successful attempt to stop Burbage's lawsuit in the King's Bench (B-3). The Court of Wards (B-4) could no longer stop the King's Bench lawsuit after the winter of 1597–98, when the Earl came of age (October 6, 1597) and sued livery. Documents: the bill (dated only Michaelmas 41 Elizabeth, evidently the winter of 1598–99), Allen's reply (after October 22, 1600), the Earl's replication (Michaelmas 1600), and Allen's rejoinder (Michaelmas 1600). In his reply, Allen gave the chronology of the events in Category B from 1596 to 1600 and also the history of how he and his father had come to own their part of Holywell (see Category A).

B-6. E.123/26/f.165^v (not yet used): An order of the Court of Exchequer King's Remembrancer of November 19, 1600. Giles Allen pointed out that Cuthbert Burbage's lease (B-2) had now run out so that the Earl of Rutland should proceed against Allen only (B-5). The court agreed. It had already stopped Burbage's lawsuit in the King's Bench (B-3).

B-7. E.123/27/f.110^v (Stopes, p. 189): An order of the Court of Exchequer King's Remembrancer of January 30, 1601. The Earl of Rutland had not proceeded in his lawsuit (B-5), so Giles Allen asked that the court dismiss it. The court gave Rutland until the end of the term (Hilary).

B-8. St.Ch.5/A.33/37 (Braines, p. 14n): A lawsuit in the Star Chamber of Trinity Term 1601 in which Giles Allen sued Thomas Screven, John Knapp, Francis Langley, and their associates for three trespasses on what he took to be his properties in Holywell. Screven's associates (John Powell, Richard Robinson, and Roger Amyes) had seized one piece of property in May 1596, and the first two and Knapp the same piece for a second time on November 2, 1597 (see B-3, 5); Langley and his associates (Amyes, John Lewis, and John Johnson) had seized another piece on May 16, 1601. Allen's lawyer supposed that the seizure of November 1597, was the first, so he described the three lawsuits earlier than this one as coming after that seizure rather than two before (B-3, 4) and one after (B-5). Allen, of course, would have known better. The lawyer also got the date of a lease between Screven and Knapp wrong (he gave it as November 1, 1597, rather than July 20, 1596), but that was probably Allen's ignorance, who had learned the right date by the time he drew up his interrogatories (B-9) for this lawsuit. Documents: bill (June 27, 1601), the reply (a demurrer) of Langley, Amyes, Knapp, and Lewis (October 17, 1601), the reply of Screven (October 20, 1601), the replication of Allen (November 29, 1602), a synopsis of Allen's replication (November 29, 1602).

B-9. St.Ch.5/A.26/1 (Braines, pp. 14, 26n): Interrogatories and depositions belonging to the lawsuit in the Star Chamber (B-8), all on Giles Allen's behalf. Allen sought to establish mainly the process by which Thomas Screven and his tenants had sublet the disputed properties. Documents: interrogatories for John Knapp, Roger Amyes, John Lewis, and Francis Langley (October 1, 1601); interrogatories for Screven (October 23, 1601), depositions of Knapp, et al. (October 26, 1601), deposition of Screven (November 10, 1601).

B-10. E.134/44–45 Eliz./Mich./18 (Halliwell-Phillipps, I, 350, 352, etc.; Stopes, pp. 189–93; Braines, pp. 5n, 13n, 14n, 16, 26n, 27): The interrogatories and depositions ostensibly for both Giles Allen and the Earl of Rutland, but actually only for Rutland (see B-11), in the lawsuit in the Court of Exchequer King's Remembrancer (B-5). Thomas Screven (in the Earl's name) tried to show, among other things, that what in Richard Manners's lease (B-1) and Webb's patent (A-3) was called the oat barn was not the barn giving onto the void ground of the 1590s, but Allen's great barn or brewhouse. Hence, presumably, the premises which the old documents gave to Allen were not the ones about which Allen was now complaining, but others to the north which were part of Allen's acknowledged domain in Holywell. Screven's witnesses, however, could not bear him out, though all had known Holywell for at least forty years and one for sixty. Documents: interrogatories (undated), a commission appointing examiners (June 23, 1602), depositions of Mary Askew,[9] Anne Thornes, Nicholas Sutton, Mary Hebblethwayte, John Rowse, and Leonard Jackson (all taken on October, 12, 1602).

B-11. E.123/28/f.270^v (Stopes, p. 194): An order of the Court of Exchequer King's Remembrancer of October 18, 1602. Giles Allen protested that he had not been ready when the court had taken depositions six days before (B-10), and that the Earl of Rutland had introduced irrelevances in his interrogatories. The court gave both sides until the end of the month to finish the depositions and ordered any irrelevances suppressed.

B-12. E.128/17/Easter 2 Jas. I/[52 from bottom] (not yet used): An order of the Court of Exchequer King's Remembrancer of April 30, 1604. Giles Allen asked the court to dissolve the injunction (see B-5) which prevented him from getting at the Earl of Rutland in the King's Bench (B-3). The court gave the Earl a week to show cause to the contrary.

B-13. E.128/17/Easter 2 Jas. I/[102 from bottom] (Braines, p. 23):[10] An order of the Court of Exchequer King's Remembrancer of May 4, 1604. On the appearance of the Earl of Rutland's lawyer (see B-12), the court ordered that the Earl's lawsuit against Giles Allen (B-5) be heard during the first sitting of the next term and in the meantime the Earl's injunction was to remain in force. (The orders for the next term are missing, and there is no order in the case in the term after that: E.128/18/Mich. 2 Jas. I.)

B-14. E-13/472/m.1 (Braines, p. 15): An entry on the Exchequer plea roll of an indenture of June 20, 1615, by which Thomas Screven's executor, Francis Gofton, sold his property in Holywell. Among the pieces sold were the disputed ones of Category B, which Gofton had had trouble selling "by reason of a title or question therevnto made by" Giles Allen's successor, Sir Thomas Dacres. So the argument went on, but Screven and then his successor seem to have had possession. Screven had died in 1613, Allen in 1608.

Category C

This quarrel took place between James Burbage and his family on the one hand and his financier's financiers and widow on

the other. When Burbage took his lease on the site of the Theatre, he had nothing like enough money to build the playhouse
and not even enough to build or renovate the other, lesser
structures on which he had engaged himself to spend £200. He
therefore took in his childless brother-in-law, John Brayne, a
successful grocer. The general understanding was that Burbage
and Brayne would own the place jointly and finance it jointly;
and inasmuch as Brayne was childless, he spoke of leaving his
half to Burbage's children in his will. It was obviously a good
bargain for Burbage, and it provided Brayne a rather exotic venture in his declining years. They got the place built, but the
cost was much greater than they had thought it would be.
Brayne bankrupted himself, and the two men fell to arguing
(sometimes violently). Neither carried out the legal steps
which he had promised: Burbage kept the lease entirely in his
own name, and Brayne did not draw a new will. Brayne's only
documentary rewards for his investment were two bonds
which he extracted from Burbage for performance of various
parts of their arrangement. There was an arbitrament in 1578
by which the two men proposed to regularize their affairs,
but they could not carry out some of its requirements.

Brayne died in 1586, and soon his widow, Margaret, and his
creditors, mainly Robert Miles, began trying in one of the
courts of common law to collect the value of Brayne's two
bonds from Burbage or (alternatively) to get title to half the
Theatre and so collect half its profits. In the fall of 1588 Burbage sued them in Chancery to get the bonds cancelled and to
stop them from making claims on the playhouse. Margaret
Brayne soon counter-sued in Chancery. The two lawsuits in
Chancery jogged on side by side for seven years. Then, with
Margaret Brayne dead and Miles carrying on by himself,
Chancery returned the case to the point at which it had begun,
when, at the Burbages' suggestion, the court told Miles to try
to collect his bonds at common law. Seven years before, the
Burbages must have feared that he and Brayne's widow might
collect them, but now, evidently, they felt safe enough. Perhaps it was one thing for the widow Brayne to sue them and
another for one of her husband's creditors to do so. In any
event, Miles did not collect the value of the bonds, and after

James Burbage died in February 1597, and the lease fell in two months later, Miles sued Cuthbert Burbage in the Court of Requests. It was fundamentally the same matter as that of the two lawsuits in Chancery, but because Burbage was dead and the lease at an end, Miles could introduce enough new matter to qualify the old matter for another court. This lawsuit disappears possibly because the documents among which it could have been chronicled are missing. Cuthbert, the son, might actually have done what James, the father, had stoutly and sometimes violently refused to do, pay Miles something for peace. Wallace, however, an ardent partisan of the Burbages, allowed no such possibility. He may have underestimated the force of the widow Brayne's case as a matter of equity, if not as one of common law (pp. 157, 158, 163).

C-1. Missing (see C-2): A lawsuit in the Court of Chancery of 1586–87 in which John Brayne's widow, Margaret, sued one of his creditors, Robert Miles. Miles was probably trying to sue her at common law for money lent her husband toward the Theatre and another of her husband's enterprises, the George Inn, Whitechapel; and she probably sued Miles in Chancery to head off the lawsuit at common law. (In any event, the widow Brayne and Miles soon gave up suing one another and joined in attacking one of the sources of John Brayne's financial troubles, his dealings with James Burbage. See Stopes, pp. 48–49.)

C-2. C.33/73/f.384ᵛ (A book) and /74/f.372 (B book) (Stopes, p. 159): An order of the Court of Chancery of May 6, 1587, in Margaret Brayne's lawsuit against Robert Miles (C-1). Miles was given a week to answer.

C-3. C.3/222/83 (Wallace, pp. 39–45; Stopes, pp. 154–59): A lawsuit in the Court of Chancery of Michaelmas term 1588 in which James Burbage sued John Brayne's widow, Margaret, and her confidant and Brayne's former associate, Robert Miles. Brayne's widow and creditors, including Miles, had been suing James Burbage at common law for two bonds which Burbage had given Brayne for performance, and (which was much the same thing) they had been publicly claiming half the Theatre. The Burbages wanted the bonds cancelled and the claims on the Theatre stopped. Documents: the bill and answer (a demurrer), both undated except that the bill has an 8 at the top as the last digit of a date, evidently 1588.

C-4. C.33/77/f.454 (A book) and /78/f.449 (B book) (Wallace, p. 46; Stopes, pp. 159–60): An order of the Court of Chancery of February 17, 1589, in James Burbage's lawsuit against Robert Miles and others (C-3). Burbage urged that Miles and the others should reply fully rather than merely demur, and the court appointed one of the Masters in Chancery, Dr. Matthew Carew, to look into the matter.

C-5. Missing (see C-6-ff.): A lawsuit in the Court of Chancery of 1589–90 in which Margaret Brayne responded to James Burbage's lawsuit of 1588 (C-3, 4) by counter-suing the Burbages (James and his two sons, Cuthbert and Richard). Documents: the bill and answer (a demurrer). (See Wallace, p. 46.)

C-6. C.33/79/f.610 (A book) and /80/f.597ᵛ (B book) (Wallace, pp. 46–47; Stopes, p. 160): An order of the Court of Chancery of May 21, 1590, in Margaret Brayne's lawsuit against the Burbages (C-5). She urged that the Burbages should reply fully rather than merely demur, and the court appointed one of the Masters in Chancery, Dr. Julius Caesar, to look into the matter.

C-7. C.33/81/f.109 (A book) and /82/f.113ᵛ (B book) (Collier, *Memoirs*, pp. 8–9; Halliwell-Phillipps, I, 371; Wallace, pp. 47–48; Stopes, pp. 160–61): An order of the Court of Chancery of November 4, 1590, in Margaret Brayne's lawsuit against the Burbages (C-5). Caesar ruled that the Burbages should answer (see C-6), and Margaret Brayne then demanded that the court collect half of the profits of the Theatre and other premises on the site. The court gave the Burbages a week to argue why it should not.

C-8. C.33/81/f.145 (A book) and /82/f.150 (B book) (Wallace, pp. 48–49; Stopes, p. 161): An order of the Court of Chancery of November 13, 1590, in Margaret Brayne's lawsuit against the Burbages (C-5). The Burbages gave reasons why the court should not collect half the profits of the property (see C-7), and the court ordered rather oracularly that both sides observe an arbitrament of July 1578. That arbitrament provided that John Brayne and James Burbage each owned half of the Theatre and other buildings, and required that the profits of the place go to pay the joint debts of Brayne and the Burbages, and after those debts were paid, go wholly to Brayne until he had been paid what he had spent above what the Burbages had spent. One of the troubles with the arbitrament now was that how much each of the parties had spent was one of the questions to be decided. Margaret Brayne regarded this order, therefore, as a victory for her, but the Burbages thought otherwise and violently defied her attempts to enforce it (see Wallace, pp. 7–8, 17–19).

C-9. C.33/81/f.270 (A book) and /82/f.280ᵛ (B book) (Wallace, p. 49; Stopes, p. 161): An order of the Court of Chancery of November 28, 1590, in Margaret Brayne's lawsuit against the Burbages (C-5). Robert Miles (Margaret Brayne's backer) swore that James and Cuthbert Burbage had defied the order of November 13 (C-8); the court ordered the Sheriff of Middlesex to attach the Burbages.

C-10. C.24/218/93 [pt. 2, halfway through the box] (Wallace, pp. 50–57): Interrogatories and depositions in the Court of Chancery on behalf of the Burbages as part of Margaret Brayne's lawsuit against the Burbages (C-5). Documents: interrogatories (undated); the depositions of John Hyde, grocer, and George Cloughe, clothworker (both December 8, 1590). The Burbages sought to discredit her husband and to establish that he had invested much less in the Theatre than she said, and hence that neither he nor she should own half of the place. (On Wallace's p. 57, line 4, "Js." should be "Jo.")

C-11. C.33/81/f.317ᵛ (A book) and /82/f.327ᵛ (B book) (Wallace, p. 49; Stopes, p. 161): An order of the Court of Chancery of January 30, 1591, in Margaret Brayne's lawsuit against the Burbages (C-5). Cuthbert Burbage had freed himself (and presumably his father, James) from the Sheriff of London (rather than Middlesex—see C-9) by bonding himself to appear in court on this day;[11] he duly appeared and so saved his bond.

C-12. C.24/221/12 [first in the box] (Wallace, pp. 57–63): Interrogatories and depositions in the Court of Chancery on behalf of Margaret Brayne as part of her lawsuit against the Burbages (C-5). Documents: interrogatories (undated); the depositions of Cuthbert and James Burbage (both February 16,

1591). She inquired into the Burbages' defiance of the order of November 13, 1590 (see C-8, 9).

C-13. C.33/81/f.456ᵛ (A book) and /82/f.455ᵛ (B book) (Collier, *Memoirs*, p. 9; Wallace, p. 64; Stopes, pp. 161–62): An order of the Court of Chancery of March 23, 1591, in Margaret Brayne's lawsuit against the Burbages (C-5). The Master of the Rolls ordered the depositions of Cuthbert and James Burbage (C-12) referred to Dr. Julius Caesar, one of the Masters in Chancery, who was to report whether the Burbages had committed a contempt of court (see C-8, 9).

C-14. C.33/81/f.493ᵛ (A book) and /82/f.497 (B book) (Collier, *Memoirs*, p. 9; Wallace, pp. 64–65; Stopes, p. 162): An order of the Court of Chancery of April 24, 1591, in James Burbage's lawsuit against Margaret Brayne and Robert Miles (C-3). The Burbages diverted attention from Margaret Brayne's lawsuit against them by pointing out that she and Miles had not yet answered James Burbage's lawsuit of Michaelmas 1588; the court again referred the matter to Dr. Carew (see C-4). (For a list of mistakes in Wallace's transcription, see p. 102 above.)

C-15. C.33/81/f.720ᵛ (A book) and /82/f.725ᵛ (B book) (Wallace, p. 65; Stopes, p. 162): An order of the Court of Chancery of June 15, 1591, in James Burbage's lawsuit against Margaret Brayne and Robert Miles (C-3). Evidently Dr. Carew had not carried out the order of April 24, 1591 (C-14); so Burbage got the court to repeat it.

C-16. C.33/81/f.818 (A book) and /82/f.831ᵛ (B book) (Collier, *Memoirs*, p. 10; Wallace, p. 66; Stopes, p. 162): An order of the Court of Chancery of July 20, 1591, in Margaret Brayne's lawsuit against the Burbages (C-5). Dr. Caesar had not been able to carry out the order of March 23, 1591 (C-13). So the Master of the Rolls appointed another of the Masters in Chancery, Dr. John Hone, to carry it out and also, if possible, to end the lawsuit, and, if not possible, to report to the court his opinion of the lawsuit and whose fault it was that he could not end it.

C-17. C.24/226/9 [pt. 2, second in the box] (Wallace, pp. 68–78): Interrogatories and depositions in the Court of Chancery on behalf of the Burbages as part of Margaret Brayne's lawsuit against them (C-5). Documents: interrogatories (undated); the depositions of Henry Bett (September 30, 1591), Giles Allen (November 3, 1591), and Bryan Ellam, Richard Hudsone, and William Clerke (all February 25, 1592). The Burbages continued trying to establish that Margaret Brayne's husband had not invested as much money in the Theatre as she said (see C-10), and hence that she should not own half of the place. (On Wallace's p. 72, line 8, "buildinge" should be "building*es*" and, line 20, "it" should be "is.")

C-18. C.24/226/10 [pt. 1, last in the box] (Wallace, pp. 78–92): Interrogatories and depositions in the Court of Chancery on behalf of James Burbage as part of his lawsuit against Margaret Brayne and Robert Miles (C-3). Documents: two sets of undated interrogatories, one for Gascoyne, Bett, and James, the other for Hynd; depositions of Henry Bett (September 30, 1591), Ellen Gascoyne (May 8, 1592), and John Hynd and William James (both July 24, 1592). Burbage tried to make the same case in this lawsuit as in Margaret Brayne's lawsuit against him and his sons (C-5), that Brayne had not invested as much in the Theatre as his widow said, and hence that she should not own half of the place. He added here that if Brayne had ruined himself, he had done so not because of his interest in the Theatre, but because of his and Robert Miles's interest in an inn, the George in Whitechapel.

C-19. C.33/83/f.16ᵛ–17 (A book) and /84/f.18ᵛ (B book) (Wallace, pp. 66–67; Stopes, pp. 162–63): An order of the Court of Chancery of October 12, 1591, in Margaret Brayne's lawsuit against the Burbages (C-5). Dr. Hone reported that the Burbages should be arrested for contempt (see C-9, 13, 16). The Burbages protested, and the court ordered that two other Masters in Chancery, Drs. Edward Stanhope and Thomas Legg, consider further whether the Burbages had committed a contempt, and in the meantime Margaret Brayne was not to take advantage of Hone's report.

C-20. C.33/83/f.151–51ᵛ (A book) and /84/f.163–63ᵛ (B book) (Wallace, pp. 67–68; Stopes, p. 163): An order of the Court of Chancery of November 13, 1591, in Margaret Brayne's lawsuit against the Burbages (C-5). Drs. Stanhope and Legg had heard both sides and recommended (with the consent of both sides) that they seek authority to put to John Hyde, Raphe

Miles, Nicholas Byshop, and John Allein (all witnesses for Margaret Brayne) such questions as both sides might propose (see C-19). The court gave authority. (In his note on p. 68, Wallace is oversimple and so misapplies three of the five sheaves of interrogatories and depositions which he mentions—C-17, 18, 21, 22, 23.)

C-21. C.24/228/11 (Wallace, pp. 92–109): Interrogatories and depositions in the Court of Chancery as part of Margaret Brayne's lawsuit against the Burbages (C-5). These are the interrogatories (undated) which Margaret Brayne drew up because of the order of November 13, 1591 (C-20), and the depositions of Nicholas Byshop (January 29, 1592), John Allein (February 6, 1592), Raphe Miles (February 10, 1592), and John Hyde (February 12, 1592). She continued to argue that she owned half the Theatre and other buildings on the site. James Burbage was wrong, therefore, to deny her half the profits and had committed a contempt in defying the order of November 13, 1590 (C-8; see also C-9, 11–13, 16, 19). (On Wallace's p. 98, line 4, "his" should be "him.")

C-22. C.24/228/10 (Wallace, pp. 109–27): Interrogatories and depositions in the Court of Chancery as part of Margaret Brayne's lawsuit against the Burbages (C-5). These are four sets of undated interrogatories (one for each witness) which the Burbages drew up because of the order of November 13, 1591 (C-20), and the depositions of John Hyde (February 21, 1592), Nicholas Byshop (April 6, 1592), Raphe Miles (April 26, 1592), John Allein (May 6, 1592). The Burbages tried to discredit the deponents and to show that Robert Miles was financing Margaret Brayne's lawsuit in return for which he hoped to own a share of the Theatre; they suggested that the Braynes' right to half the Theatre ended when the lease was mortgaged and the mortgage was not promptly paid off, so that the lease technically passed for a time to the mortgagor.

C-23. C.24/226/11 [pt. 1, first in the box] (Wallace, pp. 127–53): Interrogatories and depositions in the Court of Chancery on behalf of Margaret Brayne, part of her lawsuit against the Burbages (C-5). Documents: interrogatories (undated); the depositions of John Griggs, Edward Collyns (both July 29, 1592), Robert Miles, Henry Lanman (both July 30,

1592), and William Nicoll (July 31, 1592). She tried to establish that up to the time of his death, her husband was indeed half-owner of the Theatre and had expended great sums on it.

C-24. Guildhall, MS.9172/16/26ᵛ (the original), MS.9171/18/26ᵛ (the register copy) (Wallace, pp. 153–54): Margaret Brayne's will, made on April 8, and proved on May 3, 1593, in the London Commissary Court. She left all her possessions to Robert Miles, including her interest in the Theatre, hence her lawsuit (C-5).

C-25. C.33/85/f.758 (A book) and /86/f.785 (B book) (Wallace, p. 155): An order of the Court of Chancery of February 11, 1594, in Margaret Brayne's former lawsuit, now Robert Miles's, against the Burbages (C-5). Drs. Stanhope and Legg had been about to make their report about the lawsuit when she had died and the lawsuit ended. Since then Miles had revived the lawsuit in his name (see C-24). The court therefore ordered that Stanhope and Legg make the report that they would have made had Margaret Brayne not died. (Wallace's text follows that of the B book, unlike his usual practice; apparently he had not found the entry in the A book.)

C-26. C.33/87/f.857ᵛ (A book) and /88/f.862 (B book, perished) (Wallace, pp. 155–56; Stopes, p. 163): An order in the Court of Chancery of March 14, 1595, in James Burbage's lawsuit against Margaret Brayne and Robert Miles, now Miles alone (C-3). The Burbages pointed out that this lawsuit and the other (C-5) in which Miles was suing them were essentially the same matter, and they proposed that because Miles's lawsuit was due for hearing on May 28 and theirs ready for hearing, though unscheduled, the two should be heard together on the 28th. The court agreed with them, unless Miles could show good cause to the contrary. (For "28," Wallace misread "23.")

C-27. C.33/89/f.130 (A book) and /90/f.140ᵛ–41 (B book) (Collier, *Memoirs*, pp. 10–11; Wallace, pp. 156–57; Stopes, p. 164): An order in the Court of Chancery of May 28, 1595, technically in Robert Miles's lawsuit against the Burbages (C-5), but actually also in James Burbage's lawsuit against Miles (C-3; see also C-26). The court heard the case and agreed with the Burbages, that Miles should try at common law to collect from the Burbages the value of the two bonds which

James Burbage had given John Brayne for performance, and if he could not succeed there, then Chancery would take up the case again. (The two lawsuits in Chancery ended here, where they had begun. Miles did not collect the value of the bonds at common law, nor did he return to Chancery.)

C-28. Req.2/241/14 (Wallace, pp. 158–62): A lawsuit in the Court of Requests of between April 13 and May 9, 1597, in which Robert Miles sued Cuthbert Burbage and Giles Allen. James Burbage having died in February 1597, and the lease on the site of the Theatre having expired on April 13, 1597, Miles sued Burbage's son and heir, Cuthbert, and the owner of the property, Allen. He argued as Margaret Brayne and he had in Chancery (C-5), except that he now involved Allen, mainly because he needed to make the lawsuit different from the other in order to qualify it for another court. He urged that Allen should renew the lease, and he said that he had asked the Burbages to pull down the Theatre (as the lease entitled them to do while it was still in force) so that he and they might sell the materials and divide the money. Document: the bill only, undated.

C-29. Req.1/48/9 May 39 Eliz. (Wallace, p. 162): An order of the Court of Requests of May 9, 1597, in Robert Miles's lawsuit against Cuthbert Burbage and Giles Allen (C-28). Burbage and Allen declined to reply, arguing that this lawsuit was the same as Margaret Brayne's and Miles' lawsuit in Chancery (C-5). The court ordered that the attorneys on both sides compare the two bills and make a report.

C-30. Req.1/48/27 May 39 Eliz. (Wallace, p. 163): An order of the Court of Requests of May 27, 1597, in Robert Miles's lawsuit against Cuthbert Burbage and Giles Allen (C-28). Miles argued that this lawsuit involved different people from those in the lawsuit in Chancery (C-5; see C-29); the court agreed and ordered Burbage and Allen to reply to the lawsuit without delay. (The lawsuit disappears now, possibly because the decree and order books of the Court of Requests are missing from December 7, 1597, to April 24, 1599.)

Note. Mrs. Stopes (pp. 163–64, 164–65) noted two additional documents, an order in Chancery of June 7, 1594, and a lawsuit in Chancery, the bill dated November 13, 1594, but neither concerns the Theatre. The order is part of a lawsuit in which James Burbage sued one Gregory More: C.33/87/f.274–74ᵛ (A book) and /88./f.277ᵛ (B book). In the lawsuit, Robert Miles sued his son, Raphe, and Nicholas Byshop about the George Inn in Whitechapel: C.3/245/85.

Category D

This quarrel is about the dismantling of the Theatre and the carrying away of it to Southwark, where it became the Globe.

The Burbages' lease on Giles Allen's property at Holywell began in April 1576 and ran for twenty-one years. The lease contained a clause stating that if James Burbage spent £200 on various structures other than the Theatre within ten years, Allen would renew the lease for another twenty-one years, to begin when the renewal was signed. Burbage thought that he had spent the money, and he presented a new lease for Allen to sign in 1585. Allen refused to do so on several pretexts, mainly that the new lease was not word-for-word like the original one and that Burbage had not spent the money. Toward the end of the original lease, the Burbages offered to take another lease for twenty-one years at a higher rent and with a cash payment of £30 (which Allen said James Burbage owed for rent). Allen demanded another cash payment of £100 for repairs to the various structures other than the Theatre, which the Burbages may or may not have been willing to pay. But he also demanded that the Burbages use the Theatre as a playhouse for only five more years, after which they were to use it for some more decent purpose and eventually to pass it to Allen when the lease should run out. To this condition the Burbages and their company could not agree. So from April 1597, when the original lease ran out, until Christmas 1598, Allen suffered them to keep the property without a lease. Then in that Christmas season, they had the Theatre dismantled and carried away, as a clause in the original lease allowed them to do while the lease was in effect.

Allen, of course, by this time thought that he owned a playhouse. When he found that he owned a vacant piece of ground instead, he went smartly to law, and the Burbages and company (who must have worked it all out in advance) set about very skilfully defending themselves. Allen sued them at once (spring 1599) in the King's Bench for trespass and damage. The Burbages counter-sued Allen almost a year later in the Court of Requests, a court known for swift judgments, arguing mainly that Allen should have renewed the original lease, hence that the Burbages still had the right to take away their playhouse, and hence that the lawsuit in the King's Bench should be stopped. The Court of Requests stopped the lawsuit in the King's Bench in April 1600, heard the case on October 18, 1600, and found for the Burbages. Allen promptly (in January 1601) tried another lawsuit in the King's Bench, accusing the Burbages not of taking away the Theatre, but of having failed to keep the terms of the original lease. Then in the November following he took the Burbages to the Star Chamber, charging them with having got their verdict in Requests by various frauds. That court was looking into one of these alleged frauds in May 1602—ironically, one which even if it was a fraud would not have affected the verdict in Requests—but evidently Allen got as little comfort from the Star Chamber as he had got from Requests.[12] In 1602, therefore, three years after it had opened, the Globe was free at last of Giles Allen.

D-1. K.B.27/1362/m.587 (Halliwell-Phillipps, I, 348–49, 359–60, 361, 362; Wallace, pp. 163–80; Stopes, pp. 198–200): A summary of a lawsuit in the King's Bench in which Giles Allen sued the Burbages' builder, Peter Street, for entering "the Jnner Courte yarde" of Holywell Priory with force and arms on January 20, 1599,[13] and taking down and carrying away a building called "the Theater," worth £700. Allen filed the suit in Easter term 1599, but the summary on the King's Bench roll is dated Trinity Term 1600. (On Wallace's p. 177, three lines from the bottom, "may lawfull" should be "maye be lawfull.")

D-2. Req.2/87/74 (Collier, "Original History," p. 64; Halliwell-Phillipps, I, 348–49, 358–59, 360, 361, 362, 371–72; Wallace, pp. 180–205, 253–58; Stopes, pp. 200–16): A lawsuit in the Court of Requests in which Cuthbert Burbage sought to stop Giles Allen's lawsuit in the King's Bench (D-1). Documents: Burbage's bill (January 26, 1600), Allen's reply (February 4, 1600), Burbage's replication (April 27, 1600). Attached to these documents are interrogatories (June 5, 1600) for two of Allen's witnesses, Robert Vigerous and Thomas Nevill, their depositions (both of August 14, 1600), and a commission to examine them in the country (June 5, 1600): separated from the other documents of the kind (D-7), probably because unlike the other witnesses, these were examined in the country.

D-3. Req.1/198/Easter 42 Eliz./9 April (Stopes, p. 216): A list of witnesses of April 9, 1600, in the Burbages' lawsuit against Giles Allen in the Court of Requests (D-2), for both sides: Philip Baker, Henry Johnson, John Goburne, William Smyth, Richard Hudsone, Thomas Osborne, Thomas Bromfield, William Furnis.

D-4. Req.1/49/10 Apr. 42 Eliz. (Wallace, p. 205): An order of the Court of Requests of April 10, 1600, in the Burbages' lawsuit against Giles Allen (D-2). The court ordered Allen's lawsuit in King's Bench (D-1) stopped if on April 17 Allen could not "shewe good matter" to the contrary.

D-5. Missing (see D-6): An order of the Court of Requests of April 17, 1600, in the Burbages' lawsuit against Giles Allen (D-2). The court declared that it would hear both sides on April 22 about whether Allen should stop his lawsuit in the King's Bench (D-1). This document is missing probably because Allen challenged the stopping of that lawsuit twice, in Requests and then in the Star Chamber (D-14, 16, 17, 18).

D-6. Req.1/49/22 Apr. 42 Eliz. (Wallace, pp. 205–6): An order of the Court of Requests of April 22, 1600, in the Burbages' lawsuit against Giles Allen (D-2). As it had appointed on April 17 (D-5), the court heard arguments on this day about whether Allen should stop his lawsuit in King's Bench. The court decided that both sides should examine their witnesses by the second day of the next term (May 19) and that the whole matter should be heard on the eleventh day of the next term (May 31) "peremptorilie." In the meantime the court ordered that the Burbages reply to Allen's lawsuit in the King's Bench before Monday next (April 28), but that Allen not proceed with it himself. (For a list of Wallace's mistakes in transcription, see p. 102 above.)

D-7. Req.2/184/45 (Wallace, pp. 206–50; 259–66): Interrogatories and depositions for both sides in the Burbages' lawsuit against Giles Allen in the Court of Requests (D-2). Allen tried to show that he did not have to renew the Burbages' original lease because they had not kept its terms, and that the Burbages had agreed to a lease recently which, among other things, raised their rent, cost them £100 in repairs, and precluded their taking away the Theatre. The Burbages tried to show that they had kept the terms of the original lease and had not agreed to the recent one. Documents: Allen's interrogatories (Easter 1600); the depositions of his witnesses, Philip Baker, John Goburne, and Henry Johnson (all on April 26, 1600); the Burbages' interrogatories (Trinity 1600); the depositions of their witnesses, Richard Hudsone, Thomas Bromfield, Thomas Osborne, William Furnis, William Smyth, Randolph May, and Oliver Tylte (all on May 15, 1600); the Burbages' interrogatories (Trinity 1600) for Allen's witnesses, Johnson and Goburne, and their second depositions (both on May 23, 1600); Allen's interrogatories (June 5, 1600) for two later witnesses, Robert Miles and his son Raphe, and their depositions (both on October 1, 1600). See also D-2.

D-8. Req.1/198/Trin. 42 Eliz./23 May (Stopes, p. 216): A list of witnesses of May 23, 1600, in the Burbages' lawsuit against Giles Allen in the Court of Requests (D-2), for both sides: Oliver Tylte, Randolph May, John Goburne, Henry Johnson.

D-9. Missing (see D-11, 16–18): An order of the Court of Requests of May 31, 1600, in the Burbages' lawsuit against Giles Allen (D-2). The court did not hear the case on this day as it had appointed on April 22 (D-6), but ordered that the case be heard on the eleventh day of the next term (October 18), and, probably, that the examining of witnesses be completed early in October. In the meantime, the court ordered that Allen not proceed with his lawsuit in the King's Bench (D-1). This document is missing probably for the same reason as D-5.

D-10. Req.1/121/2 June 42 Eliz. (Affidavit Register) and /122 [uncovered volume] /2 June 42 Eliz. (Affidavit Entry Book) (Wallace, p. 251): An affidavit of June 2, 1600, by Giles Allen in the Burbages' lawsuit against him in the Court of Requests (D-2). Allen swore that he knew nothing of the depositions so far taken and that he wanted others examined on his behalf: Richard Parramore, Robert Vigerous, Thomas Nevill, Robert Miles, Raphe Miles, John Hyde, and William Gall. (Wallace's text follows /122.)

D-11. Req.1/121/11 June 42 Eliz. (Affidavit Register) and /122 [uncovered volume] /11 June 42 Eliz. (Affidavit Entry Book) (Wallace, p. 252): An affidavit of June 11, 1600, by Cuthbert Burbage in the Burbages' lawsuit against Giles Allen in the Court of Requests (D-2). Burbage swore that Allen was pressing the lawsuit in the King's Bench (D-1) contrary to the order of the Court of Requests on May 31, 1600 (D-9). (Wallace's text follows /122. On his p. 252, line 3, "Counsailo^r" should be "Counsailo^{rs}"; hence the two abbreviated nouns which follow should be expanded as plurals.)

D-12. Req.2/372/pt.I [bottom of the box] (Wallace, pp. 252–53; Stopes, p. 216): An order of the Court of Requests of June 11, 1600, for the arrest of Giles Allen because he had defied an order of May 31, 1600 (see D-9, 11), part of the Burbages' lawsuit against him (D-2).

D-13. Req.1/109/f.8 (Wallace, p. 266): A note in the Appearance Book of the Court of Requests that Giles Allen appeared in court on October 9, 1600, by virtue of the order of the court that he be arrested (D-12), part of the Burbages' lawsuit against him in that court (D-2).

D-14. Missing (see D-16, 17): An order in the Court of Requests of October 18, 1600, in the Burbages' lawsuit against Giles Allen (D-2). The court heard the case on this day and decreed that Allen should have renewed the original lease for ten years, and hence that the Burbages were right to take the Theatre down and carry it away. The court ordered that Allen stop his lawsuit in the King's Bench (D-1) permanently and not sue the Burbages about the matter again. The court also ordered that the Burbages could, if they liked, sue Allen for not renewing the original lease. The court allowed Allen just one crumb. He had charged that the Burbages had fraudulently secured the order of May 31 (D-9), which had caused him to be arrested (D-11, 12), and he was allowed now to pursue the matter—but the matter had nothing to do with the dismantling and taking away of the Theatre. The book is missing in which this order would have been entered, if it was not omitted, as D-5, 9 may have been, because Allen challenged the matter in the Star Chamber (D-17).

D-15. Missing (see D-18 and Wallace, p. 294): An order of the Court of Requests of November 1, 1600, in the Burbages' lawsuit against Giles Allen (D-2). The court ordered that the verdict of October 18 (D-14) not be signed until the court had considered further Allen's assertion that the order of May 31 (D-9) was fraudulently incomplete (see D-17). This document is missing, probably for the same reason as D-5, 9, 14.

D-16. K.B.27/1373/m.257 (Halliwell-Phillipps, I, 349, 358; Wallace, pp. 267–75; Stopes, pp. 217–19; Braines, pp. 11–12): A summary of a lawsuit in the King's Bench, begun in Hilary Term 1601, in which Giles Allen (having just lost the lawsuit in the Court of Requests—see D-14) sued the Burbages not for having taken away the Theatre, but for having failed to keep the terms of the lease on the property on which the Theatre had stood. The summary is dated Easter 1602. (On Wallace's p. 268, line 2, "ascensu" should be "assensu"; and five lines from the bottom and on p. 269, line 1, "Daridge" should be "Dotridge.")

D-17. St.Ch.5/A.12/35 (Collier, "Original History," p. 69; Halliwell-Phillipps, I, 360–61, 372; Wallace, pp. 275–90; Stopes, pp. 220–27): A lawsuit in the Star Chamber, in which Giles Allen (having lost his case in the Court of Requests [D-2] on October 18, 1600) sued the Burbages for removing the Theatre from Holywell. Allen charged that the Burbages had got the verdict in Requests (D-14) by a number of frauds, and that the order of May 31, 1600 (for violating which he was arrested), was fraudulently incomplete and hence that he did not violate it (see D-9, 11, 12). Documents: Allen's bill (November 23, 1601), the demurrer of the Burbages, their builder (Peter Street), and others (April 28, 1602), the reply of Richard Lane, the clerk who entered the order of May 31, 1600 (April 28, 1602), and the demurrer of Richard Hudsone and Thomas Osborne, two of the Burbages' witnesses (June 12, 1602). (On Wallace's p. 287, line 20, "ther" should be "then.")

D-18. St.Ch.5/A.33/32 (Wallace, pp. 290–97): The interrogatories (May 1, 1602) for Richard Lane and his deposition

(May 11, 1602), part of Giles Allen's lawsuit in the Star Chamber against the Burbages (D-17).

Note. Mrs. Stopes (p. 219) included an additional document, K.B.27/1373/m.260, a summary of a lawsuit in the King's Bench in which Giles Allen sued John Knapp for trespassing apparently on the property in Holywell. The summary follows immediately that of D-16 on the King's Bench roll, but the matter does not concern the Theatre, because the trespass occurred in January 1602, three years after the removal of the Theatre from Holywell. A John Knapp was one of Screven's associates against Allen in 1601 (B-6).

Notes

1. Published among *The Shakespeare Society's Papers*, iv, 63–70.
2. See *History of English Dramatic Poetry to the Time of Shakespeare* (London, 1879), iii, 257 ff.
3. Wallace, *The First London Theatre: Materials for a History* (Lincoln, Nebr., 1913), in University Studies, xiii, 1, 2, 3 (January, April, July 1913); and Stopes, *Burbage and Shakespeare's Stage* (London, 1913). See his waspish notes about her (pp. 45, 276) and her pained notes about him (pp. ix–x, xii–xiii and note).
4. "The Site of 'the Theatre,' Shoreditch," *London Topographical Record* xi (1917): 1.
5. Wallace wrote a footnote (p. 31) to show that he knew about Category B and did not think it very important. Unintentionally, he also showed that he had not given it much attention. He alluded to a series of matters belonging to it, all but three of which Halliwell-Phillipps had found, especially in one document (B-10), and quoted extensively without giving a citation. Wallace mentioned the document but cited only Halliwell-Phillipps. The other three matters (Francis Langley and lawsuits in Wards and Star Chamber) can most conveniently be found in either of two documents, B-8 or its dependent, B-9, an important part of Category B which Halliwell-Phillipps had not found. Evidently Wallace had found one of these documents or both and little else. He cited neither, but he assured his readers that the important parts of Category B would take "their due place in the final presentation," a work which he did not live to write.
6. I count only clear mistakes. One could find many more if he were to insist on absolute rigour. Many of the Wallaces' mistakes were probably the result not of transcription but of proofread-

ing, which somebody in Lincoln did while they were in Europe (p. 39), and which must have been a nightmare to do. For all 2,050-odd lines at which I looked, the Wallaces made one mistake in seven or eight as they printed them.

7. The Wallaces were strangely prone to mistranscribing signatures, as those of James Burbage (p. 63), John Goburne (p. 218), Richard Hudsone (p. 229), and William Smyth (p. 239).

8. No one was fined as a result of the lawsuit, for there is no estreat of fine in E.159 for any of the people in it.

9. Her name at the beginning of her deposition is not easily legible. In answer #2, she said that she was once the wife of "Roberte Farrer." So Mrs. Stopes called her "Mrs. Farrar." Braines (p. 16), however, read her name at the beginning of her deposition correctly as "Marie Askew."

10. Braines used the document correctly in his article in the *London Topographical Record*, p. 10n, but he left it out of his part of the *Survey of London*, VIII, and misread and misapplied it in 1923.

11. Confusion about sheriffs of London and Middlesex occurred because the two sheriffs of London served jointly as sheriff of Middlesex.

12. There is no estreat of fine in E.159 for the Burbages or Richard Lane; hence they were probably not fined in Star Chamber.

13. See my article above, pp. 32–35.

INDEX

Adams, J. Q.: *Shakespearean Playhouses*, 50, 101
Agas, Ralph: View of London, 75n15, 95n16
Allein, John (actor, 1592), 20, 28n5, 35, 37, 38, 39, 40, 123
Allen, Christopher, 29, 105–6, 107, 114
Allen, Giles, 17–19, 25, 26, 29, 31, 32, 33, 34, 36, 38, 39, 40, 41, 101, 105–6, 107–16, 122, 125, 126–32
Allen, John (Yeoman of the King's Bears, 1552), 93n3
Alleyn, Edward, 20, 35, 94n9, 95n17
Amyes, Roger, 110, 111–12, 113, 114–15
Anglo, Sydney: *Spectacle, Pageantry, and Early Tudor Policy*, 61, 64, 72
Askew, Mary, 116

Baiting: rings, x, 75n15, 81–87; ape-baiting, 85, 89; bear-baiting, 82, 84–87, 88–89, 90, 92, 94–95n16; bull-baiting, 84–87, 88–89, 92, 94–95n16; *see also* Beargarden
Baker, Philip, 128, 129
Banqueting halls, x, 1; at Ardres (1520), 77n34, 79n41; at Calais (1520), 60–74, 77n28; at Paris (1518), 78–79n41
Beargarden, 83–84, 87–88, 89–93, 93n3, 95n17
Bel Savage inn, 48
Belknap, Sir Edward, 60–61
Berry, Herbert: "The Playhouse in the Boar's Head Inn, Whitechapel," 3
Bett, Henry, 122
Bevis (a bull), 87

Blackfriars playhouse, 13, 17, 26, 98
Boar's Head playhouse, 3, 13, 47, 97, 111–12
Braines, W. W.: *The Site of the Globe Playhouse*, 99; "The Site of 'The Theatre,' Shoreditch," 99–100, 104, 105–6, 108
Braun, G. and Hogenberg, Frans: View of London, 85–86, 95n16, 96(fig.3)
Braye (a smith), 38
Brayne, John, 18–22, 25, 26, 27nn2–4, 29, 31, 35, 36, 39, 40, 41, 42, 82, 101, 116–18, 119–20, 122, 123, 124, 125
Brayne, Margaret, 28n3, 29, 35, 36, 37, 44n38, 116–17, 118–25
Bromfield, Thomas, 43n3, 103, 128, 129
Browne, John, 60
Bumpsted, Christopher, 105–6, 107
Burbage, Cuthbert, 29, 30, 31, 32, 33, 34, 35, 36, 38, 39, 40, 44n36, 44n39, 82, 100–101, 105, 108, 110–14, 117, 118–25, 126–32, 133n12
Burbage, Ellen, 29, 33
Burbage, James, x, xi, 3, 13, 17–22, 24–27, 27n3, 28n5, 29, 30, 31, 32, 35, 36, 37, 38, 39, 40, 41, 42, 73, 81, 82–84, 93, 100–101, 105, 110–14, 116–26, 126, 129, 133n7
Burbage, Richard, 29, 30, 31, 33, 34, 35, 36, 38, 44n36, 82, 100–101, 105, 110–14, 117, 119–24, 126–27, 130–31, 133n12
Byshop, Nicholas, 123, 126

Caesar, Julius, D.C.L., 119, 121
Calais, 47, 60, 78n41; exchequer, 62,

77n28; staple hall, 62; *see* Banqueting halls
Carew, Matthew, D.C.L., 119, 121
Cecil, Sir Robert, 22, 25
Chambers, E. K.: *Elizabethan Stage*, 22, 24, 38, 45n43, 74n2, 100, 104; *William Shakespeare*, 20, 21
Charles v, 60–62
Clerke, William, 122
Cloughe, George, 120
Clyomon and Clamydes, 14n16
Cockpit-in-Court theatre, 3
Collier, J. P.: *Memoirs of the Principal Actors in the Plays of Shakespeare*, and "Original History of 'The Theatre' in Shoreditch," 97–98, 100, 104
Collyns, Edward, 123
Cornish, William, 60
Court of Aldermen, 20
Cross Keys inn, 48
Cupolas: at the Theatre, Globe i and ii, 52, 55, 56
Curtain playhouse, ix, 2, 3, 4, 12, 13, 17, 19–27, 31, 39, 40, 48, 49, 50–53, 76n17, 84, 91, 95n18; "esore" at, 17–27

Dacres, Sir Thomas, 116
Dahood, Roger, 77n32
Dee, John, 88
Devon, F., 98
DeWitt, Johannes: drawing of the Swan, 2, 4, 5, 8, 32, 48, 49, 50, 52, 54, 73, 75n8, 77n26, 82, 89, 90
Disguising house: at Greenwich (1527), 78n39
Doors: of playhouses, 36, 55; of playhouse galleries, 36, 49; in tiring house façade, 50, 74–75n8

Ellam, Bryan, 30, 122

Faithorne, William and Newcourt, Richard: View of London, 75n15
Farrer, Robert, 133n9
Farringdon Without, ward of, 22, 24
Faunte, Sir William, 87
Fencing: at playhouses, 50, 92
Field, John, 88, 89
Field of the Cloth of Gold, 60
Finsbury Fields, 47

Fisher, Sidney, 50–53
Flags: of playhouses, 52–53, 56
Flagstaffs: of playhouses, 52–53, 55–56
Fleetwood, William, 20, 25
Fortune playhouse i, ix, 2, 47, 50, 56, 91; contract for, 49, 50, 60, 73, 76n21
Fortune playhouse ii, 2
Foundations: of playhouses, 30, 59, 90, 91, 96(fig.3)
Foxe, John: *Book of Martyrs*, 7
Francis i, 77n34, 78–79n41
Frens, Dale, 64
Furnis, William, 43n3, 103, 128, 129

Gall, William, 130
Galleries: of the banqueting house, Calais, 61, 63, 66–67, 69–70, 73; of the banqueting house, Paris, 79n41; of the Beargarden, 87–88, 95n18; of playhouses, 35, 36, 37, 44n32, 48–49, 54, 55, 56, 58, 89, 91, 95n18, 96(fig.3)
Gascoyne, Ellen, 122
Gatherers: at the Theatre, 36, 49
George inn, Whitechapel, 118, 122, 126
Gibson, Richard, 60
Globe playhouse i, ix, 26, 27, 32, 33, 35, 56, 57, 59, 60, 76n21, 91, 99, 101, 111, 126–27
Globe playhouse ii, ix, 2, 47, 48, 55, 56, 59–60, 76–77n26
Goburne, John, 103, 128, 129, 133n7
Gofton, Francis, 116
Goodgame, John, 108
Greene, Robert: *Comical History of Alphonsus, King of Aragon*, 9–11
Greene, Thomas, 26
Greenwich, 22–23, 24
Griggs, John, 123
Guisnes, Castle of, 60, 61

Hall, Edward, 60, 78n37
Halliwell-Phillipps, J. O.: *Outlines of the Life of Shakespeare*, 98, 100, 104, 132n5
Harbert, Thomas, 25
Harvey, Gabriel, 48
"Heavens," x, 2, 3, 4, 5, 6, 7, 8, 8–12, 95n18; machinery in, x, 2, 3, 4, 6,

8–12, 55, 56; throne in, 5, 11
Hebblethwayte, Mary, 116
Henry VIII, 47, 60–62, 78n39, 111
Henslowe, Philip, 2, 3, 4, 6, 9, 12, 13, 25–26, 32, 41, 82, 83–84, 94n9
Heywood, John: *The Play of the Weather*, 9
Hickes, Richard, 24
Hill, Richard, 111
Hodges, C. Walter, xi; *The Globe Restored*, 74n5, 82, 83; *Playhouse Tales*, 76n21, *Shakespeare's Second Globe*, 60
Hollar, Wenceslaus (Wenzel): Long Bird's-Eye View of London, 49, 55, 59–60, 73, 76n20
Holinshed, Raphael: *Chronicles*, 77n31, 78n37
Hollingworth, John, 108
Holywell (Halliwell), 82; lane, 24; priory, 106, 107–16, 126–27, 132
Hone, John, D.C.L., 121, 122
Hope playhouse, ix, 2, 3, 47, 50, 55, 56, 75n15, 88, 89, 90–92; contract for, 49, 55, 73, 83, 91
Hotson, Leslie: "This Wooden O," 50; *Shakespeare's Wooden O*, 50
Hudsone, Richard, 30, 122, 128, 129, 131, 133n7
Huts: above the stage, 52, 55–56, 56, 59, 73
Hyde, John, 18–19, 41, 120, 122–23, 130
Hynd, John, 122

Innyards, x, 1, 20, 84, 88

Jackson, Leonard, 116
James, William, 122
Johnson, Henry, 36, 128, 129
Johnson, John, 111, 114–15
Jones, Inigo, 3, 50

Katherens, Gilbert, 90
Kelley, James, 108
Kiechel, Samuel, 44n33, 48, 55, 74n2
King's Men, 26, 56, 77n21
Knapp, John, 110, 111, 114–15, 132
Kyd, Thomas: *Spanish Tragedy*, 6, 7
Kynesbury, Warks., 22

Lambarde, William, 88, 89
Lambeth, 94n9
Lane, Richard, 131–32, 133n12
Langley, Francis, 13, 25, 84, 111–12, 114–15
Langley, Jane, 25
Lanman, Christopher, 23
Lanman, Henry, 17, 19–27, 28nn3–4, 31, 39, 40, 123
Leacroft, Richard: *The Development of the English Playhouse*, 81, 83
Legg, Thomas, D.C.L., 122, 124
Lewis, John, 111, 114–15
Linnell, Rosemary: *The Curtain Playhouse*, 76n17
Lodge, Thomas and Greene, Robert: *A Looking Glass for London and England*, 8, 9, 11
Lord Admiral's Men, 11, 20, 37
Lord Arundel's Men, 20
Lord Chamberlain's Men, 56, 57, 74n8, 81
Lords' room, 50; *see also* Rooms
Lyly, John, 5; *The Woman in the Moon*, 9

Magno, Allessandro, 88, 89
Manners, Sir Richard, 109, 112–13, 115
Marlowe, Christopher, 4; *Dr. Faustus*, 4, 8
May, Randolph, 30, 103, 129
Merian, Matthew: View of London, 76n20
Middleton, Thomas: *A Game at Chess*, 77n26
Miles, Raphe, 29, 39, 40, 41, 44n32, 103, 122–23, 126, 129, 130
Miles, Robert, 27–28nn2–3, 29, 33, 36, 37, 39, 40, 41, 44n38, 102, 103, 117–26, 129, 130
Mill, J. S., 92
Monro, Mr., 98
More, Gregory, 126

Nevill, Thomas, 128, 130
Newcourt, Richard: View of London, 75n15
Newington Butts playhouse, ix, 2, 4, 5, 12, 24, 37
Nichols, J. G.: ed., *The Chronicle of Calais*, 77n32

Nicoll, William, 124
Norden, John: Views of London, 3

Orrell, John, 75n9
Osborne, Thomas, 42n3, 128, 129, 131

Paris Garden, Manor of, 25, 84, 85; map of, 75–76n15
Parr, Queen Katherine, 106
Parramore, Richard, 130
Payne, William, 83, 87–88, 89, 93n3, 95n18, 96(fig.3)
Peckham, Edmund, 29, 38, 105–6, 107–9
Peckham, George, 29, 105–6, 107–9, 112
Peele, George: *Battle of Alcazar*, 8
Play of Daniel, The, 12
Pope, Thomas, 26
Poulter, Simon, 93n3
Powell, John, 110, 113, 114–15
Preston, Thomas: *Cambysis, King of Percia*, frontispiece, xi
Profits: of playhouses, 36–42; of playhouse galleries, 41–42
Public Record Office, 98–99, 100

Queen Anne's Men, 26
Queen Elizabeth's Men, 8, 20–21

Rastell, John, 60
Robinson, Richard, 110, 113, 114–15
Roofs: of playhouse galleries, 30, 31; over stages, *see* "Heavens"
Rooms: in playhouses, 36, 48–49
Rose playhouse, ix, 2, 3, 5, 6, 9, 12, 13, 25–26, 32, 41–42, 48, 56, 82, 83, 84, 91
Rowe, William, 108
Rowse, John, 116
Rutland, Earls of, 109–11, 112–16

St. Mary Woolchurch Haw, 23, 24
Samwell, Richard, Sr., 13, 112
Sanuto, Marino, 62–64, 65–73, 78n41
Savage, Jerome, 24
Savoy, Duchess of, 62
Screven, Thomas, 29, 110–16, 132
Seats: in playhouses, 70, 73
Shakespeare, William, ix; *R2*, *Rom.*, *MND*, *MV*, *Jn.*, 74n8

Smith, Irwin: "Theatre into Globe," 57–60
Smith, William (fl. 1568–75): *A breffe description of . . . London* and *A Particular Description*, 86–87, 94n12, 95n16, 96(fig.3)
Smyth, William (fl. 1599), 33, 128, 129, 133n7
Southwark (incl. Bankside and St. Mary Overy), 32, 33, 57, 75n15, 82, 85, 101, 126
Stages, 4, 49, 50, 55, 56, 72–73, 74, 89, 91, 95n18, 96(fig.3); curtains (hangings), 74–75n8; discovery space, 74–75n8; inner stage, 1; machinery, *see* "Heavens"; pillars or posts, x, 2, 3, 4, 5, 6, 6–8, 12; traps, 2, 3, 4; upper station, 74–75n8
Stairs: in playhouse galleries, 36, 49, 54–55, 56, 59, 73
Stanhope, Edward, D.C.L., 122, 124
Stockwood, John, 48
Stopes, Charlotte C.: "The Burbages and the Transportation of the Theatre," 76n21; *Burbage and Shakespeare's Stage*, 98–105, 125, 132
Stow, John, 77nn31–32; *Chronicles of England*, 61, 70, 77n31, 78n37
Street, Peter, 2, 4, 33, 57, 58, 76n21, 127, 131
Stubbs, Philip, 48
Stuckley, William, 96n2
Sutton, Nicholas, 116
Swan playhouse, ix, 5, 13, 25, 47, 48, 49, 54, 56, 76n15, 77n26, 84, 91, 111; drawing of, *see* DeWitt

Thornes, Anne, 116
Tiltyards, 90
Tiring houses, 35, 49, 50, 74, 74–75n8, 95n18
Turpin, Richard: *The Chronicle of Calais*, 61–62, 64–73
Tylte, Oliver, 103, 129

Underwood, John, 26
Urmeston, Clement, 60–61

View of the City of London (University of Utrecht), 47, 50–56
Vigerous, Robert, 128, 130

Visscher, J. C.: View of London,
76n20

Wallace, C. W.: *The First London
Theatre*, 5, 20, 22, 23, 38, 98–105,
118, 123, 132n5, 133n7
Wallace, Hulda, 98–99, 102
Webb, Henry, 105, 109, 111, 113, 115
White, Thomas, 48
Wickham, Glynne: *Early English
Stages*, 92, 93n5
Wilson, Robert: *The Cobbler's
Prophecy*, 9; *Three Lords and Three
Ladies of London*, 6, 7, 8
Winchester, Bishop of, 95n17
Windows: in playhouses, 36, 55
Wistowe, Robert, 83, 88, 93n3, 94–
95n16
Woodliffe, Oliver, 13

Yards: of playhouses, 35, 36, 37, 49,
91; of the banqueting house, Calais,
73; of the Beargarden, 88